DENBY D
AND
UPPER DENBY

Unknown and Unseen

DENBY DALE AND UPPER DENBY

Unknown and Unseen

RARE PHOTOGRAPHS AND DOCUMENTS
FROM PRIVATE ARCHIVES

Chris Heath

Pen & Sword
LOCAL

First published in Great Britain in 2017 by
PEN AND SWORD LOCAL
an imprint of
Pen & Sword Books Ltd
47 Church Street
Barnsley
South Yorkshire
S70 2AS

ISBN 978 1 52671 933 1

A CIP catalogue record for this book is available from the British Library

Typeset in Times New Roman by Chic Graphics

Printed and bound in England by CPI Group (UK) Ltd, Croydon, CR0 4YY

Pen & Sword Books Ltd incorporates the imprints of
Pen & Sword Aviation, Pen & Sword Family History, Pen & Sword Maritime,
Pen & Sword Military, Pen & Sword Discovery, Wharncliffe Local History,
Wharncliffe True Crime, Wharncliffe Transport, Pen & Sword Select,
Pen & Sword Military Classics, Leo Cooper, Remember When,
The Praetorian Press, Seaforth Publishing and Frontline Publishing

For a complete list of Pen & Sword titles please contact
PEN & SWORD BOOKS LIMITED
47 Church Street, Barnsley, South Yorkshire, S70 2AS, England
E-mail: enquiries@pen-and-sword.co.uk
Website: www.pen-and-sword.co.uk

Contents

Dedication

This book is for all the wonderful people who have helped to create a fantastic archive for the Denby Dale and district area. Whether they loaned photographs, passed on information, aided with family history or made available their sizeable collections of memorabilia to me or provided technical aid, I am proud to have known them all.

This book is also dedicated, as was my very first one back in 1997, to my dad, though now sadly it is in his memory. It was my dad who encouraged me to research the family tree aged around 12, how big now is the oak tree grown from that little acorn? Thanks Dad, maybe see you again some time.

Acknowledgements

Robert Gaunt; Tony, Ann and Adam Turton; Catherine Hobbes; Patricia France; Charles Hewitt; Jonathan Wilkinson; Sylvia Menzies; Paul Heath; Linda Senior.

*   *   *

Any errors or omissions are entirely the fault of the author. Whilst every effort has been made to trace the copyright owners of the illustrations in this book, the author wishes to apologise to anyone who has not been acknowledged. If an error has occurred, this will be corrected in any subsequent reprint of this work.

Introduction

As this is my eleventh book covering some of villages in the Upper Dearne Valley there may be some among my loyal readers who might wonder if there is anything left to say. It has been awaiting publication for some time as I have held off lest more lost photographs or documents emerge. I find it both immensely frustrating but frankly astonishing when something unusual comes up for sale or is passed on to me and I am always thankful to donors who take the time and the trouble to do so.

This volume is a kind of union between my Denby & District series of books and the Ye Olde Township volumes. The breadth and scope of the villages covered is smaller and the emphasis is very much more on Denby Dale and Upper Denby. These are the villages where I was born, raised and have lived, and the reason for my interest and pursuit of their history and that of the people who over the centuries have made them.

After many hundreds of thousands of words and many hundreds of photos across my previous works I feel I've got to know some of these people and if I take a walk through the churchyards at Upper Denby or Cumberworth I am not just looking at the words carved into a tombstone. In the vast majority of cases I have come across the individuals named and know something of their lives in old records and sometimes even know what they looked like in life. I'm not saying they were all good, but they are, at least, familiar. I feel that with this book I have returned home.

After the photographs sections, which are all published for the first time, there then follows a sort of notes and queries chapter. It follows a chronological timeline but much (certainly the more ancient documents) would have been better to have been included in a Denby & District book. Sadly, these new discoveries will have to stand on their own, as it would be wrong to start repeating myself in order to create a background for them. Of course, I would recommend that for those interested you get hold of previous volumes and familiarise yourselves with the centuries concerned.

There are numberless families who have ancient roots in the area that could be researched and published in some form, but in this volume, I have concentrated on three: the Gaunt family of Upper Denby, which still existed until very recently; the

Turton family of doctors and surgeons; and the Senior family of Denby Dale, as a mark of respect to an old friend who is no longer with us.

The biggest surprise with this volume comes with the details of the Denby Dale branch of the Royal British Legion. In all my years researching I have never come across any mention of the society. Indeed, the present-day headquarters of the Legion had no knowledge of it either, but that has now been corrected and the branch lives on again. During the sifting of records I came across notes relating to a group photograph of the committee being taken and reproduced in significant numbers and an enlargement being made to go on the wall of the hut. If only one of these had survived then I would have included it though if any readers know of a copy I could borrow, then please contact me via the publisher.

The Denby Dale and Upper Denby brass bands were once vital components of village life (and competitive ones at that), taking part in village festivals, carnivals, fetes, gigantic pies, Christmas events and suchlike, and deserve to be remembered as much more than my previously published photographs of them. And this partial record of their competition entries addresses at least some of this issue.

Finally, the Upper Denby Club. This stood opposite my family's home until it was demolished and the records for it are sparse, indeed, I appear to have the only ledger to have survived. I was greatly surprised to find the name of my grandfather as a member throughout its duration, as indeed were my father and uncle, who had no idea that he had joined in the venture. This just goes to show that no matter how much research is undertaken, however many paths of enquiry are followed up, there is always something new to discover. So, in answer to my question at the beginning of this introduction, yes, there is plenty left to say and plenty more to find out.

Chris Heath
February 2017

Rare and Unseen Photographs from the Archives

Barnsley Road heading towards Catchbar, with the lane heading up to Toby Wood on the left. Circa 1940.

Carr Bridge, Denby Dale. This was a favourite beauty spot for taking photographs during Victorian and Edwardian times such as this.

Demolition of the old wooden viaduct taking place during 1884, taken from Barnsley Road.

A typical view of the Denby Dale viaduct after snowfall. Circa 1930s.

An excellent view of the village. The allotments opposite Dearne Terrace are apparent, along with Kenyon's Dearneside Mills and Hillside.

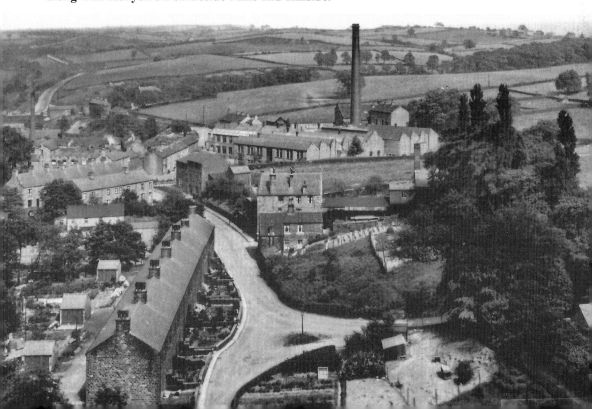

Taken from the viaduct, this vantage point remained a popular way to photograph almost the entire village. Dearne Terrace is to the left and Norman Road can be seen snaking its way towards Wakefield Road above it. Dearneside Mills are to the right with Springfield Mills in the top centre.

Another photograph taken from the top of the viaduct, this one looking straight down Wakefield Road. Kitson's premises are to the left abutting Polygon Terrace.

A view of the Wesleyan Chapel and Manse before the building of the Victoria Memorial Hall. The large sycamore tree to the right was cut down prior to construction taking place. Circa 1890s.

A further view of the Wesleyan Methodist Chapel, Manse and Wesley Terrace leading up to them. The Victoria Memorial Hall, to the right, began construction in April 1903 and was officially opened on 11 June 1904 as a Sunday School attached to the Wesleyan Chapel. Circa 1920.

Crowds begin to arrive for the opening ceremony of the new Salvation Army building on 4 December 1926. The guest of honour was local dignitary Sir James Peace Hinchliffe. The Salvation Army had begun in Denby Dale in a wooden hall near the centre of the village on 11 September 1884. Its first officer was Captain Mary McIver. The founder of the movement, General William Booth had visited Denby Dale in 1907 and was heard by large crowds. Meetings were to be held in this new hall until 1970, when the corps was disbanded.

Sir James Peace Hinchliffe, in the centre of the photograph in front of the doors, flanked by other dignitaries and members of the Denby Dale Salvation Army Corps, young and old, on the occasion of the opening of the new hall on 4 December 1926. Sir James (1862-1933) was the son of the Denby Dale mill founder Zaccheus Hinchliffe.

An unknown parade on Wakefield Road, largely made up of male youths. They are passing the village school to the left. Circa 1920s.

Withyside, Denby Dale, taken around the 1930s. The fields behind were later to become the Gilthwaites housing estates, also including Rockwood Rise, Woodside, Greenside, Thorpes Avenue and others.

An unknown village parade on Wakefield Road, the ladies are passing the bottom of Leak Hall Lane with Victoria Terrace in the background. Circa 1930s.

WAKEFIELD R⁹, DENBY DALE

Wakefield Road, probably 1940s. The shop to the left has survived to the present, though is now a part of the Londis group. To the right is the Denby Dale Garage. The signs are advertising Dominion Petrol. The garage survived until the late 1990s, when it closed and the Brook Meadows housing estate was built.

Clough Cottage at Lower Putting Mill. A document dated 1851 informs us that at that time there were four cottages in total, three of which had once been a fulling mill.

Bank House, formerly the home of the Kenyon family, one of the three major mill-owning families in Denby Dale, taken from Church Fields with the mill dam in the foreground.

Taken from the back of the terraced houses on High Street, this shot is looking up through the gardens towards the viaduct. Circa 1940.

Taken from the back of the houses on High Street (now Wakefield Road, which stand opposite the Dale Inn). This snow scene looks out onto houses at the bottom of Bank Lane and includes, to the very top left, the buildings at Inkerman Mill, complete with chimney. Circa 1940.

This rare photograph shows the view up Norman Road towards the main Wakefield Road. To the right is a general store that was known locally as 'Nippers'. The reason for this is that the one-time proprietor was scrupulously careful to never knowingly give anything away for free and that he would nip a pea in half in order to get the correct weight for the money. Circa 1900.

Norman Row, at the bottom of Norman Road, opposite Springfield Mill. Note the gas lamp. Circa 1910.

Dearne Terrace on Bank Lane, with at least sixteen people posing for the photograph. Circa 1910.

Dearne Terrace again. The houses were built by the Hinchliffe family as homes for members of their workforce. Circa 1910.

The Tin Chapel built in 1893 in the shadow of the viaduct, which was superseded in 1939 by the stone-built church that survives today. The chapel continued in use as a church hall and dances were held there at times during the mid-twentieth century.

Cottages on Dearneside Road, opposite Kenyon Bank, formerly the site of Kenyon's Mill. Circa 1900.

Woodlands House on Dearneside Road, the former residence of the Denby Dale village doctor. Circa 1920s. The practice used to operate at the building on
Wakefield Road, which is now home to the newsagent.

Denby Dale School and the master's house, which opened in 1874, taken prior to the Second World War.

With the passing of time and the lack of recording, it is almost impossible to name any of the people in the following school photographs. It is certain they are all taken at Denby Dale and they are included here for completeness and for the strong sense of the past that they evoke.

Above, Denby Dale mixed class, Mr A Turton is the master on the left and Wilfred Barnes the headmaster to the right. Wilfred Barnes arrived at the school in 1875 and retired in 1903. The photograph probably dates from the late 1880s.

15

A similar photograph to the latter one and most likely taken on the same day. Wilfred Barnes appears to the right once again. Circa late 1880s.

A mixed group of children with two female teachers in the playground. Circa 1900-1910.

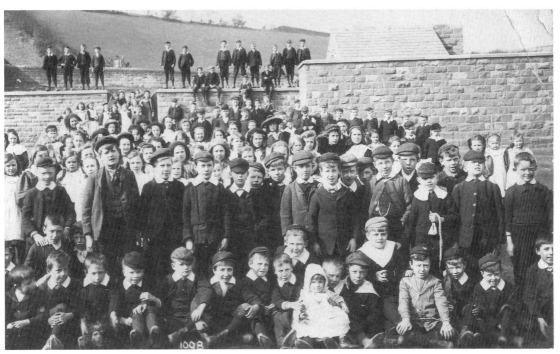

The entire school (minus teachers) pose for a photograph in the main playground. It would seem likely that some parents were around as the female toddler in white seated on what we can only presume was her brother's knee is too young to be a pupil. The photograph is dated 1907 and simply says 'love to all from all at Denby Dale'. It was sent to St Ives, perhaps to a former teacher, though maybe slightly tongue in cheek as she is addressed as 'Mrs Noall'.

Another mixed group with an unknown master to the left. Circa 1900-1910.

Another mixed group or class with their mistress to the left. Circa 1900-1910.

Denby Dale District Class D. The teacher to the right in spectacles is Dora Heath or Miss Heath as she would have been referred to. Dora was born in 1895 and died in 1946 aged only 51, she was at Denby Dale School for a few years before moving on to other teaching establishments. Circa 1915.

Denby Dale Infants, Class B, with three of their tutors. Circa 1900-1910.

18

This beautiful photograph shows eleven of the girls in the school yard with their teddy-bears. Curiously, the bears all look exactly the same, which means that either the school provided them or the shop in Denby Dale didn't exactly have a great choice. Circa 1905-1915.

Another class in the school yard. The teacher to the right was Miss Elsie Heath. Elsie was the sister of Dora and both were the daughters of Hugh and Caroline Heath of High Street, Denby Dale. Circa 1915.

A rare interior photograph of a class in what was the main hall. The piano can be seen upon the stage to the right. Circa 1915.

Denby Dale schoolchildren in about 1936. Only three of the pupils have currently been identified. Eighth from the left on the back row is Joyce Dickinson. Third and fourth on the second row are Ethel Schofield and Dorothy Lockwood.

Denby Dale Primary School in 1954 or 1955.
Back row: Teacher (unknown), ?, S Pell, S Woodhead, I Thackra, ?, ?, P Hyde, A Wood, V Schofield, D Bostwick, ?,
Middle row: J Cook, K Wadsworth, G Morris, A Fisher, J Coppin, R Smith, E Greaves, S Ryan, C Birks, R Birks, ?, B Sharpe.
Seated: K Hirst, S Simpson, K Booth, J Hobson, M Wilkinson, M Wood, C Euston, S Ball, S Schofield, V Firth.

Denby Dale schoolchildren pictured at the Wakefield Road premises just prior to the move to Gilthwaites in 1976.
Back row, left to right: Mrs Carter, Chris Heath, Phillip Towey, Ian Jackson, John Watson, Lee Greensmith, Dean Jackson, Robert Smith?
2nd row: Susan Cocking, Hannah ?, Maria Lockwood, Rachel Brook, Ruth ?, Emily Dickinson, Paul Guest.
3rd row: ?, Linda Robinson, ?, Hannah Beevers, Joanne Hill, ?, ?.
Floor: Rupert Gill Martin, Richard Gawthorpe, ?, Simon Gill Martin, William Dunk, Kenton Mosley, John Beaumont, Barry Moody.

Denby Dale schoolchildren after the move to new premises at Gilthwaites after Easter 1976.
Back row, left to right: ?, Robert Howell, Kenton Mosley, William Dunk, Paul Guest, Barry
Moody, Richard Gawthorpe.
2nd row: Mark Brocklesby, Michelle Exley, Ian Jackson, John Beaumont, Chris Heath, ?,
Graham Higson, Linda Robinson.
3rd row: Mrs Pat Wright, Bernadette Guy, Joanne Summerville, ?, ?, ?, Mrs Butterfield.
Floor: Jeremy Bacon, Mark Mathewman, Ruper Gill Martin, Harvey Walker.

This photograph is believed to be of plate-layers working on the railway at Denby Dale. Plate-
layers had the responsibility of inspecting and maintaining the track, its rails, sleepers, bolts
and suchlike. They also greased the points and kept a careful watch for any wear and tear.
During the heyday of steam-power, a plate-layer would, typically, be assigned a mile or two
of track to look after and would have a small hut as a shelter and working base. This would
have contained chairs, a table and a simple stove. When sections of the track needed more
intensive work, teams of plate-layers would work together. Circa 1890s.

A team of plate-layers, again believed to be at Denby Dale, one of whom, to the left, is named as Jonathan Crossland. Circa 1890s.

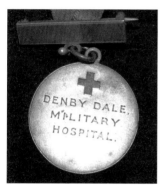

An example of the badge worn by members of the Voluntary Aid Detachment Nurses who looked after injured First World War servicemen at the Victoria Memorial Hall in Denby Dale during its conversion to a Military Auxiliary Hospital from 12 December 1916 until 28 February 1919.

The back of this badge/medal has been inscribed by its owner, Miss E Heath, who we met earlier, as a teacher at Denby Dale School.

Elsie Mary Heath, aged about 20 in 1913. Elsie never married and died in 1965 aged 72.

Elsie Heath in her VAD
uniform with the badge
clearly visible. Circa 1916.

Dora Heath, Elsie's younger sister,
also in her VAD uniform, around
1916 when she was 21.

Elsie and Dora Heath at the back
of their home on High Street along
with their step-sister Winnie (who
was to become a full-time nurse)
and their mother Caroline.

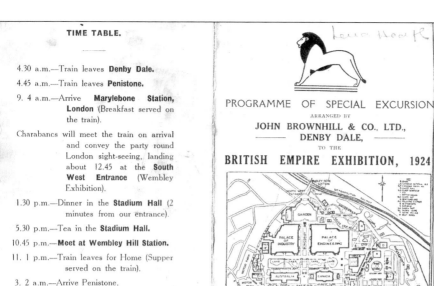

4.30 a.m.—Train leaves **Denby Dale.**

4.45 a.m.—Train leaves **Penistone.**

9. 4 a.m.—Arrive **Marylebone Station, London** (Breakfast served on the train).

Charabancs will meet the train on arrival and convey the party round London sight-seeing, landing about 12.45 at the **South West Entrance** (Wembley Exhibition).

1.30 p.m.—Dinner in the **Stadium Hall** (2 minutes from our entrance).

5.30 p.m.—Tea in the **Stadium Hall.**

10.45 p.m.—**Meet at Wembley Hill Station.**

11. 1 p.m.—Train leaves for Home (Supper served on the train).

3. 2 a.m.—Arrive Penistone.

3.15 a.m.—Arrive Denby Dale.

TIME WAITS FOR NO ONE.
BE PROMPT.

PROGRAMME OF SPECIAL EXCURSION

ARRANGED BY

JOHN BROWNHILL & CO., LTD.,
—— DENBY DALE, ——

TO THE

BRITISH EMPIRE EXHIBITION, 1924

MONDAY, SEPTEMBER 8th, 1924.

The programme produced for John Brownhill & Co, weavers in Denby Dale, for an excursion to the British Empire Exhibition at the Empire Stadium (later Wembley Stadium). The exhibition had been opened by King George V on 23 April 1924 (St. Georges Day).

SUGGESTIONS HOW TO SEE THE EXHIBITION.

In order to visit the principal exhibits, and to avoid loss of time, we recommend the following route, starting from the **South West Entrance** or the **Stadium Hall.**

1.—**Australia.**
2.—**New Zealand.**
3.—**Palace of Arts** (Queen's Dolls' House)
4.—**Palace of Industry.**
5.—**Palace of Engineering.**
6.—**Canada.**
7.—**Gold Coast.**
8.—**South Africa** (then back to **Burmah**).
9.—**India.**
10.—**Over London Bridge.**
11.—**Hong Kong.**
12.—**H.M. Government Pavilion.**
13.—**The Amusement Park.**

To get a bird's eye view of the Exhibition grounds take either

The Railodok - 2/- per person.
or
The Never Stop Railway - 6d. per person.

REMEMBER.

1.—Not to lose your **5 Tickets.**

2.—To carry with you full particulars of your name and address, and also mark the paper **" Brownhill's Party."**

3.—To keep your Identification Ribbon pinned on your left arm.

4.—There are Cloak Rooms near the South West Entrance.

5.—There are 3 Ambulance Stations in the Grounds (for Casualties) which before leaving for home will be visited.

6.—To beware of **Pick-pockets.**

7.—All Minerals, etc., at Dinner and Supper are extras, and must be paid for individually.

The inside of the programme for the British Exhibition. Of the fifty-eight countries that comprised the British Empire at the time fifty-six took part with displays and pavilions. It cost twelve million pounds to put on and was the largest trade exhibition ever staged anywhere in the world. It attracted 27 million visitors and cost 1s 6d for an adult entry and 9d for children. It was certainly a long day out for weaver Lena Heath, whose programme this was.

25

The Denby Dale & District ARP wardens during the Second World War. This photograph is taken almost at the top of Norman Road. Only two of them can currently be named. The man in the middle row, third from the left, is chief warden William Herbert Senior, who became a highly respected local historian for Denby Dale. The other is the man in the back row to the extreme right. This is Upper Denby joiner and undertaker Joe Willie Heath.

Almost exactly a replica of the previous photograph but now all the wardens have donned their gas masks. Note the bags that the gas-masks were carried in are more prevalent than the earlier picture.

A meeting of the Senior members of the Civil Defence during the Second World War, William Senior can be seen seated in the third row eleven from the left.

This pastoral scene was taken at Toby Wood Farm, probably around 1920. The lady in the photograph may be Hilda Lodge, wife of the farmer Joseph Lodge. The Lodge family were prevalent at Emley from around the mid-eighteenth century. They were certainly at Toby Wood Farm from the time of James Lodge (1860-1943) as he was buried at Cumberworth. The family was also very involved with the burial of the infamous 1887 Denby Dale Pie. The last member of the family to farm here was Tom Lodge, who remained until he retired and sold it on, moving to be nearer his family at Selandine Nook. From the age of about 40, Tom began breeding the working Shire horses on the farm and established a stud business. He went on to become a highly respected judge at country shows. Indeed, the Thomas Lodge Cup was named after him in his honour. He died in 2012 just prior to his 90th birthday.

Another photograph taken at Toby Wood Farm. It is marked 'Ms A Lodge', and this could be the sister of farmer Joseph Lodge who was born in 1897.

Lodge Family Tree

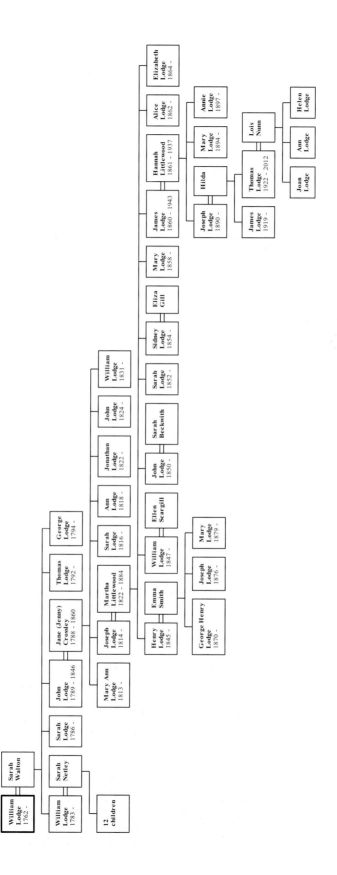

A final photograph taken at Toby Wood Farm, this of a reputed 43-stone pig.

Denby Dale & District Lay Preachers Association members, taken 2 May 1896.

A Sunday School gathering on Sunny Bank in Denby Dale in 1906.

A mid-1950s village carnival. Part of the parade is pictured here on Sunny Bank heading towards the cricket field. Betty Ryan is the woman on the extreme right in the dark coat.

Wesleyan Reform Sunday School, taken at the Zion Chapel on Barnsley Road. Circa 1930s.

A Salvation Army gathering in front of the new hall, probably during the 1940s.

The Horn family of Prospect Terrace, Wakefield Road, Denby Dale. Back, left to right: Blanche, Ida, Grace, Lena, Gladys and Ethel Horn. Front, left to right: Ava, Harry, Annie and Minnie Horn. In total, Harry and Annie had nine children (Mabel died as an infant) and all were girls. Circa 1939.

Land Girls Go To "Front Line"

Two hundred members of the Women's Land Army left London yesterday for Kent, the "front line" county. Some took tin hats, expect to be bombed. Another 300 will follow in a few days.

The girls will work in gangs, threshing Kent's part of this year's record corn crop. Many are from mills and factories in the North and have never before done any land work.

News Chronicle pictures here were taken at the station. Above are Blanche Horn (waving) and her sister Ava, from Denby Dale, near Huddersfield. Left: Vera Collet, of Manchester, and Rose Blythe, of Deptford.

Kent War Agricultural Committee will employ the girls, who will work on farms within a six-miles radius of their billets.

When threshing is in full swing 2,000 members of the Land Army will be working in Kent.

A newspaper cutting from 1940 showing two of the Denby Dale Horn sisters departing by train from London to Kent to work in the Women's Land Army.

An all-female garden party held at Rockwood House, home of Herbert Gordon Cran and his wife Dorothy, in 1916.

A further photograph of the all-female garden party held at Rockwood House in 1916. Besides the very bored-looking dog, the women are the same as those pictured in the previous photograph and still knitting. It is possible the event was held in support of the men of the village away on active service during the First World War and that the socks they produced were to end up on the front lines in France, Belgium and elsewhere.

34

Frank Kitson of Denby Dale in full military uniform, having his photograph taken between 1914 and 1918.

The 1928 Denby Dale pie preparing to take its place in the parade around the village whilst other vehicles assemble nearby to take theirs.

The old Denby Dale pie dish (used in 1887 and 1896) was always a popular place to take a snapshot, here at the junction of Sunny Bank and Miller Hill. This photograph was taken during or before 1940, when the dish was sent as scrap to be melted down and used in the war effort. Note the Salvation Army building in the top left of the picture.

An unusual view of William Wood ceremonially opening the 1928 Denby Dale pie.

MAIDEN VOYAGE OF THE "S.S. DENBY DALE 1964"

The 1964 publicity stunt when the pie dish was floated at Mirfield.

Some of the 1964 Denby Dale pie servers pose for a photograph, with many eager diners looking on.

British Rail train services and prices produced especially for the 1964 Denby Dale pie day festivities.

A view looking up Wesley Terrace during the 1964 Pie day celebrations. Pictured is Carol Newby posing with two exotic arboreal visitors for the day. It is unknown what their opinion of the pie was.

The 1980 Denby Dale carnival fancy dress competition entrants in the 7 to 11-year-old category. Taken in the cricket field, some of those competing are Janet Brisby, Paul Heath and Graham and Steven Higson.

A very old view of the Junction Inn (now the Dunkirk) who sold Brook & Co Fine ales. Circa 1890.

Two old cottages on Smithy Hill opposite the village green. These were condemned and then demolished in 1973. The car in front was a restoration and the picture was taken about 1970. The two women in the doorway are ex-Postmistress and shopkeeper Annie Heath and her sister Lena Nicholson. Their nephew, Bryan Heath, can be seen to the extreme right in front of what was once the family shop.

The house once known as Spion Cop, probably named after the battle that took place during the second Boer War in 1900 that resulted in a British loss. The view looks towards the New Inn and on to Rattan Row and Bank Lane. Circa 1910.

25th Dec 1927. Denby Church

Upper Denby Church taken from Fall Edge Lane on a white Christmas Day in 1927.

The photographer has walked a little further down Fall Edge Lane. Upper Denby School is visible to the left, with the church in the centre and the vicarage on the right. Christmas Day 1927.

The (then) newly erected grave of the former vicar of Upper Denby, Romeo Edwin Taglis, who died in 1926 aged 67 and who had been the vicar here for thirty-two years. Note the grave is against the wall facing the eastward-looking graves of the parishioners.

There are very few photographs of the one-time village shop in Upper Denby. On Smithy Hill and facing towards what has become today's village green, the window is being washed in order for customers to be able to see the items on offer in the window. Circa 1940.

Ruth E Storer, known as 'the girl preacher', who arrived with her family in Upper Denby due to her father being posted there as the village policeman shortly before 1911.

Elizabeth Heath, nee Barraclough, the one-time Upper Denby postmistress and shopkeeper and widow of its founder Harry, up a ladder inspecting damage to the stable roof behind the shop, aged over 80. Circa 1945.

Ivy Bank, Ingbirchworth, home to Benjamin Beever. Benjamin, known as Benny, was the head of a well-known firm of builders, he had eight sons and a daughter and twenty-three grandchildren. He was killed in a traffic accident in 1964 travelling back from taking part in a television programme publicising the 1964 Denby Dale pie. Only a month prior to this he had invited the entire population of Ingbirchworth to Ivy Bank to celebrate his 86th birthday, and nearly 200 people turned up.

An old view of Gunthwaite Dam, likely to have been taken in the 1930s.

The Tudor barn at Gunthwaite Hall in around winter 1950. In recent years, some timbers from the barn have been examined using dendrochronology and a date of 1560-1587 has been discovered for the felling of the trees.

Upper Cumberworth School feast 1909.

An aerial view of Beanlands Spring Grove Mills in Clayton West, probably taken during the 1940s.

A further aerial view of Spring Grove Mills, this time probably during the 1960s.

Common Side at the top of Clayton West, taken around 1910.

An R Beanland delivery vehicle taking part in a mid-twentieth century carnival in Scissett.

Cumberworth Road, Skelmanthorpe, prior to the First World War. The Garrett buildings can be seen behind the land that has become the village car park.

CUMBERWORTH ROAD, SKELMANTHORPE.

Commercial Road, Skelmanthorpe. Circa 1920s.

Grove Corner, Skelmanthorpe. Circa 1940s.

Elm Street, Skelmanthorpe. Circa 1930s.

Mill-hands at Cuttlehurst, 1910. Back row: Lucy Tipler, Mary Kendal, Lily Swalez, Ethel Wood, Edith Barraclough, Ruth Annie Beaumont, Laura Barraclough. Front row: Isaac Barraclough, Alice Bincliffe, Ivy Shillitoe, Herbert Higson, Annie Hardcastle, unknown.

The Sovereign Inn at Lane Head taken just prior to the onset of the First World War.

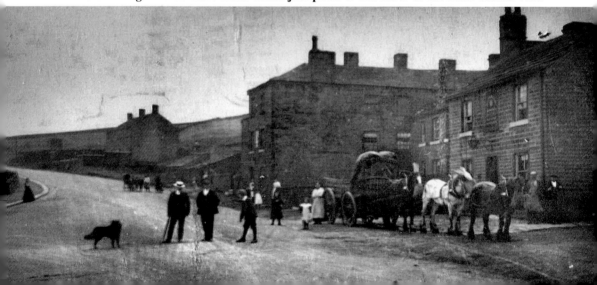

𝔄 𝔥𝔦𝔰𝔱𝔬𝔯𝔦𝔠𝔞𝔩 𝔐𝔦𝔰𝔠𝔢𝔩𝔩𝔞𝔫𝔶
1343–1812

This section contains material that would have been more in context in a Denby & District book. New information will continue to be discovered as more and more records are explored and translated, but I believe the following will prove interesting reading to anyone fascinated the area:

Aymer Burdet, Lord of Denby.
Fined for breaking into Isabella Fitz William's Park at Emley.
18 May 1343 Westminster

*Commission of oyer and terminer to John Darcy 'le cosyn', Hugh de Hastynges, William Deyncourt, Richard de Wylughby and William Basset, on complaint by Isabella late the wife of William le Fitz William that Nicholas de Worteley 'chivaler,' Nicholas his son, John de Beaumound, 'chivaler,' Thomas his brother, **AYMER BURDET**, Henry de Lacy, Adam de Hopton, James de Eland, parson of the church at Tankeresley, Roger de la Wodhalle, parson of the church of Derfeld, John de la Woodhalle, Thomas de la Woodhalle, Adam de la Woodhalle, Hugh de Eland, Robert Cursoun, parson of the church of Hicleton, and others **broke her park at Emeleye, co. York, hunted therein, carried away her goods as well as deer from the park and assaulted her men and servants, whereby she lost their service for a great time.** By fine of 20s at the instance of the Bishop of Carlisle. York.*

This wasn't to be an isolated incident by a member of the Burdet Lords of Denby as in 1395 Aymer's eldest son, Nicholas can be found doing exactly the same thing.

Inquisition post mortem of Godfrey Bosville of Gunthwaite

Godfrey Bosville (the first member of the family to settle at Gunthwaite and the builder of the magnificent black and white timber barn) died on 22 July 1580. As was customary at the time, an inquisition after death had to be held. This tradition was carried out upon the death of any of the king's tenants-in-chief and was formally known as an Escheat. The procedure was performed by the Royal Escheators appointed to each county and was made for royal financial reasons. The earliest inquisition post mortem was made in 1236 and the practice was abandoned at the start of the English Civil War, around 1640. It was formally abolished by an Act of 1660. The document allows us to get a glimpse of how much land and how many buildings Godfrey was in possession of when he died:

> *Manor of Gunthwaite with 3 messuages, 2 cottages, 1 watermill, 200 acres of land, 100 acres of meadow, 100 acres of pasture and 30 acres of wood (held of George, Earl of Shrewsbury, of his Manor of Brierley).*

> *Manor of Oxspring with 1½ watermills, 3 cottages, 200 acres of land, 100 acres of meadow, 200 acres of pasture, 20 acres of wood and underwood, 100 acres of heath and firze (gorse) and £6 6s 8d rent in Oxspring, Roughbirchworth, Thurlstone, Hunshelf and Ormethwaite (similarly held of the Earl of Shrewsbury).*

> *Capital messuage, 40 acres of land, 20 acres of meadow and 60 acres of pasture in Keresforth (held of the Crown Manor of Barnsley).*

> *In Cawthorne, 8 messuages, 2 cottages, 100 acres of land, 80 acres of meadow and 200 acres of pasture (held of Thomas Watson of Walton esq.).*

> *In Penistone, Manor of capital messuage, 3 messuages, 4 cottages, 60 acres of land, 60 acres of meadow, 100 acres of pasture and 200 acres of heath and firze (held of the Crown Manor of East Greenwich).*
> *In Barnsley, 4 messuages, 4 crofts, 20 acres of land, 10 acres of meadow, 20 acres of pasture and 100 acres of moor (held of the Crown Manor of Barnsley and sometime property of Pontefract Priory.*

Godfrey Bosville recites in his will that his eldest son and heir Francis Bosville was then over 17 years and 3 months in age.

Godfrey Bosville died on 22 July 1580.

Consistory court case 20 January 1585 to 31 October 1588
Regarding tithes of Penistone Parish (wheat, oats, sheep, wool, cattle, hay)
Participant – Richard Wortley (Plaintiff) Armiger
Participant – Henry Burdet (Defendant) Gentleman

Witnesses:

Name	Age	Abode	Occupation
John Marshall	60	Denby	Husbandman
John Marshall	67	High Hoyland	Milner
John Nebb	60	Darton	Husbandman
John Jenkinson			
John Blackburn	60	Penistone	Yeoman
Nicholas Holme	64	Clayton West	Husbandman
Thomas Woodcock	77	Normanton	Husbandman
Richard Burdet			
Randulph Burdet	37	Silkstone	Gentleman
Thomas Jenkinson	24	Denby	Yeoman
Randulph Jenkinson	64/67	Barugh	Yeoman
John Micklethwaite	68/70	Ingbirchworth	Yeoman
Thomas Cudworth	68/70	Silkstone	Yeoman
Robert West	60	Denby	Husbandman
Randulph Wadsworth	60	Penistone	Husbandman
William Wadsworth	60	Penistone	Husbandman
William Casson	54/55	Penistone	Yeoman/Domestic
Servant			
William Wadsworth	50/52	Penistone	Yeoman
William Wadsworth	64	Water Hall, Penistone	Yeoman
John Caldwell	68	Silkstone	Husbandman
James Dyche	60	Emley	Husbandman
Richard Brook	40	High Hoyland	Tanner
Matthew Hayther	72	Warmfield	Yeoman
Thomas Hayther	35	Normanton	Husbandman
William Percy	60	Darton	Yeoman
John Gomersal	60	Carlton	Yeoman
Randulph Gillet	47	Penistone	Husbandman
Peter Haworth	42	Wheatley Hill	Yeoman
John Haworth	47	Penistone	Yeoman
John Hoyle	44	Penistone	Tailor

NB: Wadsworth should actually read Wordsworth.

The Consistory Court was a kind of Ecclesiastical Court, particularly within the Church of England. Established by William the Conqueror, they still exist today, although since the mid-nineteenth century their powers are much reduced. Henry Burdet was still the Lord of the Manor of Denby at this time and was still living at Denby Hall during the period 1585-1588. His first wife, Elizabeth Jackson, had been dead for around ten years and he had by now taken up a relationship (though he never married) with Dowsabell Casson, which produced a number of illegitimate offspring. His eldest son by Elizabeth, and heir apparent, Richard, would have been around 35 and, by now, married to Mary Bosville of the Gunthwaite Bosville family. It is tempting to speculate that the reference to William Casson might acknowledge the presence of Dowsabell's brother in the area. The result of the above case is currently unknown, although plainly, Richard Wortley felt that Henry Burdet was not paying his fair share of tithe money.

George Sedascue

This gentleman is discussed in *Denby & District III* after noting his signature on the petition created by the people of Denby in support of two women accused of being witches there in 1674. Further information has now come to light about him.

During the same year that Sir William Dugdale appeared at the Star Inn, Barnsley (1665/6), to take cognizance of the arms of county families, Mr Sedascue of Gunthwaite is named among the contumacious who refused to appear. Sir George Sedascue was a Bohemian gentleman who, during the Civil War, came to England and offered his sword to Parliament, which was accepted. He afterwards settled at Gunthwaite and gave £20 towards the erection of the schoolhouse at Penistone. He died in 1717.

It was most likely that Colonel Godfrey Bosville had a hand in Sedascue's decision to settle at Gunthwaite, both being Parliamentarian soldiers.

Jan Georg Sadowski (a Pole) whose name when Latinized became Johannes Georgious Sadowski, who was known in England as George Sedascue. He was born in 1612 in Germany, the son of a Lord. The suffix '-ski' in any case indicates a noble family, and his father was evidently titled. Perhaps George himself was. The Sadowskis were Protestants, and as such would have supported the King of Sweden's occupation of Poland. They would inevitably have experienced persecution by the Catholic majority in Poland and were forced into exile. It was in 1656, the year the Polish Catholics rose violently against the Swedes and Protestants, massacring them and destroying their estates, that Sadowski's last remaining Polish property or relations would have been lost. This would explain why it was in that year that he finally sought and obtained naturalization as an Englishman. Since Cromwell had personally espoused the cause of the Polish Protestants, Sadowski's naturalization was facilitated. Equally, Sadowski may to some degree have been personally responsible for the attitude of Cromwell on this question. Sadowski's testimony was crucial in exposing Anthony Weldon as mentally ill and in vindicating Livesey.

Anthony Weldon was a courtier and politician who was disgraced and dismissed from King James I's service for various reasons and became an avid Parliamentarian during the English Civil War. Sir Michael Livesey was a puritan and a Parliamentary commander during the English Civil War. He was also one of the fifty-nine signatories on the death warrant of King Charles I.

Sadowski temporarily lost his commission in 1647.

His connection to Gunthwaite was initially brought about by his friendship with parliamentary colonel Godfrey Bosville, through whom he met Godfrey's daughter Mary and married her. The pair lived at Gunthwaite for many years. Indeed, the nonconformist minister and diarist Oliver Heywood (1630-1702) recorded that he dined at Gunthwaite with Major Sedascue in 1666. Mary's brother and the heir to Gunthwaite, William Bosville, was born in 1620 so we may speculate she was born during the 1620s, though her date of death is currently unknown. George Sedascue died in 1688 at Heath Hall, Wakefield.

We can find George Sedascue in records pertaining to Gunthwaite:

3 May 1672
Contract for Sale until 20 October 1674 at £4 5s an acre: George Sedascue of Gunthwaite, Gent., to Lionel Copley of Wadworth, Esq., Springwood in coppice called Margery Park (70 acres): Provisions for charcoaling.
Witnessed by: George Barnby and Thomas Blake.

Margery Park (Wood) is to the North of Cawthorne and abuts High Hoyland.

20 November 1676.
Lease for a year: John Shirt of Cawthorne to Godfrey Bosville of Gunthwaite, esq. Tithes of the Window Fields.
Witnessed by: George Sedascue and Timothy Kent (the Curate of Denby chapel).

1684
Draft Assignment and Letter of Attorney: George Sedascue, now of Heath to Godfrey Bosville of Gunthwaite, Esq. The contract for sale of 3 May 1672 mentioned above and all its benefits: Recites that George Sedascue acted therein for Godfrey Bosville, then an infant.

This record implies that Sedascue had only recently moved to Heath and as we have seen died four years later.

> **5 March 1717**
> *Acquittance: John Ramsden, schoolmaster of the Grammar School of Penistone (with the consent of Elkanah Rich, John Wood, William Fenton, George Walker, John Micklethwaite, Gents. And Edmund Hough, Vicar of Penistone, feoffees of the school), to William Bosvile of Gunthwaite esq.*
>
> *For £20 under the will of George Sedascue, Great Uncle of William Bosville by marriage, for the benefit of the Master of the school. Further to a recited order under a Commission for Charitable uses (5 December 1715).*

There are nine witnesses and 'fifteen principle [*sic*] inhabitants' of Penistone who sign as agreeing to the payment.

> **An appeal against an Order of Remand dated 1812**
> ***The Justices of the Peace***
> *Upon hearing the appeal of the churchwardens and overseers of the poor of the parish, township or place of Cumberworth Half in the West Riding of Yorkshire, against an adjudication order for the removal of William Burdett, and Sarah, his wife, from the township of Denby, in the said Riding, to said parish, township or place of Cumberworth Half. It was ordered by the sessions, that the said order of removal be confirmed, subject to the opinion of the Court of Queen's Bench upon the following case.*
>
> *The examination respecting the settlement of the said William Burdett and Sarah, his wife, whereon the order was made was the following:*
>
> *This examinant, William Burdett maketh oath and saith that he is sixty nine years of age and the place of his settlement is at Cumberworth Half in the said Riding, which he gained by apprenticeship with Amos Burdett, of Gilfits, in Cumberworth Half aforesaid. When I was about fourteen years of age I was put out an apprentice by 'covenant indenture' to the said Amos Burdett for the term of seven years to learn the trade of a clothier and I went to and resided with the said Amos Burdett in Cumberworth Half under the said indenture for five years and six months when my brother, Joseph Morton purchased my time out with my master for the sum of two guineas which was paid by my*

Mother, and the indentures were destroyed, and I have never done any act since, whereby to gain a settlement. I was married at Louth in Lincolnshire, to my wife, Sarah Roberts, in the year 1795. On hearing of the appeal, as soon as the respondents had opened their case, the appellants objected, that the said examination was insufficient on the face of it, and that the said order of removal ought on that ground quashed. The grounds of insufficiency relied on under the grounds of appeal which properly then pointed out were, that the alleged indenture of apprenticeship was neither shown to have been produced before the justices who took the said examination but nor its loss or destruction sufficiently shown to let in secondary evidence before the said justices of such indenture; and that if a sufficient foundation were laid in the said examination to warrant the reception of such secondary evidence, then that the secondary evidence given respecting the said indenture was wholly defective and insufficient in the following respects; that is to say that it did not appear by the said examination whether the said William Burdett was a parish apprentice, or by whom he was bound, or who were the parties to the supposed indenture; and that if he were a parish apprentice it did not appear by the said examination whether the said binding was allowed by justices of the peace; and that it did not appear the said examination either that the money given or contracted for in relation to such apprentice was inserted in the said indenture or that the indenture was duly stamped in pursuance of the statutes in force at the time when it was executed. The court of quarter sessions. After hearing evidence on both sides upon the alleged insufficiency of the said examination, overruled the objections taken and held the examination good. The appellants after such decision of the court conceded that the respondents could prove the settlement stated in the examination and that settlement was taken as proved. The appellants then proposed to rely on a subsequently acquired settlement as stated in the following, which was the seventh ground of appeal. That subsequent to the said alleged apprenticeship in our said township of Cumberworth Half (that is to say) in or about the year 1812, the said William Burdett, the pauper, rented a cottage or tenement of the value and for the sum (which he paid) of one pound ten shillings per annum, situated at Exley Gate, in your said township of Denby, in which he resided for the term of one whole year at the least, and the said pauper has ever since continue to reside and does in fact now reside at the same cottage at Exley Gate aforesaid; and that in or about the year aforesaid and at the same time that he occupied and resided in the said cottage or tenement at Exley Gate aforesaid, he also rented and occupied another tenement at Denby Hall, in your said township of Denby consisting of the keeping or feeding of a cow of which he was the owner, by and on the land and premises of James Haigh, of Denby Hall aforesaid, for the space of one whole year and which was the value of 10/. a year, at the least and for which the said pauper paid to the said James Haigh the sum of four shillings a week during the whole year, whereby the said pauper did acquire a settlement and is now legally settled in your said township of Denby. The respondents upon this admitted that the facts stated in the said seventh ground were all true; and it was agreed by the counsel on both sides that evidence sufficient to establish the said seventh ground of appeal should be taken as having been advised by the appellants, but the counsel for the respondents objected that the said seventh ground of appeal did not show upon the face of it a legal settlement in the said township of Denby. After hearing this question argued, the court of quarter sessions decided that the said seventh ground of appeal did not show upon the face of it a legal settlement in the said township and therefore confirmed the said order of removal subject to the opinion of the court of Queen's Bench.

The Gaunt Family of Upper Denby and Australia

Doctor Matthias Gaunt

In previous works I have tried to follow in the footsteps of local people who left Denby and Yorkshire for Australia. Some, like members of the Wood family of Denby Dale, went in search of their fortunes with the chance to discover gold. Others went less willingly, such as Elijah Hinchcliffe of Cumberworth, who was transported in 1841 for attempting a burglary. Every case is different and each has its own merits as a story to tell. Matthias Gaunt was born in Denby in 1793 and made the journey down-under in 1830, but before we explore his history and achievements, we must examine the family from whence he came, based in and around Gunthwaite and Denby.

The Gaunt family of Upper Denby and environs

The name Gaunt is most likely a locational name from the town of Ghent in Flanders. During the Early Middle Ages, many skilled craftsmen and wool workers left Ghent bound for England, leading to an upsurge in the number of families carrying the surname in England. There were significant numbers in and around Leeds and Leek, amongst other places. It is also possible that the name derives from the Middle English word 'Gant', meaning literally gaunt, thin, haggard or thin or slender. The best-known man to have borne the name in English history was John of Gaunt (actually John Plantagenet 1340-1399), the third son of King Edward III. He was called 'of Gaunt' because he was born there and has no relationship with the Denby families bearing the name. As an aside, the last woman to be executed in England for a political offence was Elizabeth Gaunt in 1685. She was burnt at Tyburn for her treason in sheltering the supporters of James Scott, 1st Duke of Monmouth, during his rebellion against King James II, which ended in defeat at the Battle of Sedgemoor in 1685.

The Denby branch of the Gaunt family may not have the same national history as the latter but they were established in and around Denby during the mid-1600s at least and were on-lookers as the village developed right through until the twenty-first century. We find Robert Gaunt (born about 1635) and his brother Thomas (1640-1702) living in the area during the mid-seventeenth century, and it is possible they had a sister named Maria christened at Penistone in 1633, the daughter of William Gaunt. Information regarding these individuals is at best, scant. Thomas is recorded at Stubbings, a farm bordered by 'Gaunts Wood'. The most likely site for this is Stubbing Farm off Dobroyd Hill near Denby Dale. The farm buildings have in recent years been converted into modern housing, but photographs of the buildings as they were appeared in *Denby & District III*. Thomas married Susanna Ward in 1661 at either Penistone or Kirkburton and had at least two children: Mary (in about 1662, who went on to marry Robert Wordsworth of Penistone, who was a distant relation to William, the poet of the same name) and Sarah (in about 1664). It is possible that Susanna was related to the non-conformist firebrand Ralph Ward, who was a curate of the chapel of Denby during his early career. He was born in Denby in 1629 and was preaching at Denby during 1649/50. Thomas and Susanna may have had further children, but she must have died relatively young as we can find Thomas re-marrying in 1688 to Mary Broadhead. The last mention of Thomas is in his will dated 1701, in which he mention's his brother, Robert.

It is unclear as to whether Robert also farmed at Stubbing, but it seems far more likely that he resided at Gunthwaite Gate Farm. It is through Robert that all the later generations of the Gaunt family in Denby are descended. Before we move on to later generations, it is of interest to note that both Thomas and Robert signed a petition raised by the villagers of Upper Denby in 1674 in support of two women accused of witchcraft. Thomas is also recorded in the Hearth Tax returns of 1672, where he is listed as having two hearths. Strangely, Robert is not mentioned but there was a currently unknown William Gaunt who had one hearth.

Robert and Susanna had two sons, Joshua (1660-1730) and Jonathan (1665-1725), and it is through Joshua that we can find the descent leading to Doctor Matthias Gaunt who emigrated to Australia.

The family descended from Jonathan Gaunt
Jonathan makes a note in his will (dated 1724) that he was a shoemaker. He married Judith Moxon and began a family in 1697 with the birth of his eldest son, William. William became associated with Gunthwaite Gate Farm, but it is not known whether he inherited it from his Uncle Joshua, who had sons of his own. William and his wife Tamar Marsh had at least nine children, one of whom, Mary, married Delariver Burdett, a farmer at Dry Hill, Lower Denby, and a descendant of the old lords of the manor of Denby. As the generations increased, the number of different families grew and the name Gaunt proliferated, not only in Upper Denby but in many of the nearby villages. The same names were handed down from generation to generation,

and so it was that Joshua, Jonathan, Mary, John, Joseph, Ann, Sarah and William (amongst others) feature so many times in the parish registers and other records. Some of the elder sons took over the family farms, as tenants of Lord Savile of Thornhill, but many earned their livings in the textile industry and its associated occupations. The family name was still well-represented in the twentieth century. James Henry Gaunt was financially influential with the building of the first cricket pavilion at Denby, he was also a noted photographer. John Gaunt (1852-1935) lived at 3 Ratten Row (a property owned by Denby joiner and undertaker Joe Willie Heath – amongst others), and other members of the family occupied at least one if not two further houses in the row. It seems likely that John's son John Thomas Gaunt (1885-1945) took on the tenancy after his father died. John Thomas married Mary Beldon in 1918. She was the daughter of the Beldon family of farmers at Broad Oak, Gunthwaite. Fittingly, if you take a stroll today down Gunthwaite Lane towards the old family farm of Gunthwaite Gate, you will find two wooden seats, one on each side of the road commemorating Albert Victor (Vic) Gaunt, who died in 1987. He was the brother of the above-named John Thomas.

One of a number of Gaunt family graves in Upper Denby churchyard. This one notes the burial of Joseph Gaunt 1760-1850.

John Gaunt of Upper Denby (1852-1935) the father of eight children including John Thomas and Albert Victor. The photo was taken at 3 Rattan Row, a house he rented from village joiner and undertaker Joe Willie Heath. Sadly, the name of the dog is unknown.

John Thomas Gaunt and his wife to be, Mary Beldon, probably taken in the old orchard at Broad Oak Farm, which was run by the Beldon family at this time. Circa 1918.

John Thomas Gaunt and Mary Gaunt, nee Beldon. Circa 1920.

John Thomas Beldon, Mary Gaunt, nee Beldon, John Thomas Gaunt and Charlotte Milnes (who married John Thomas Beldon) seated. Circa 1918.

The wedding party of John Thomas Gaunt and Mary Beldon. Mary is in the centre of the group of five women seated, with Charlotte Milnes to her left. The boy kneeling to the left is Stuart Gaunt (John Thomas's younger brother). John Thomas is stood behind Mary with John Thomas Beldon looking over his shoulder. Circa 1918.

Charlotte Beldon, Marian Gaunt, nee Webster, Mary Gaunt behind the seated John Beldon. Circa 1944.

Charlotte Beldon,
Mary Gaunt, Bertha
(Aspinall?) and
Albert Victor Gaunt
after the wedding of
Vic and Bertha
around 1962.

John Gaunt, the son of John Thomas and
Mary, on his own wedding day in 1944 when
he married Marian Webster. John was at first
aided by and then joined the Denby Dale
branch of the British Legion after the Second
World War.

John Gaunt with his two sons, David and Robert, at
Ingbirchworth Reservoir during a particularly dry
spell, which saw the water reduce to a level low
enough to expose the old footbridge in 1955.

The family descended from Joshua Gaunt
Joshua Gaunt (1660-1730) married Ann Thickett and they had at least five children, the eldest of whom was Joseph (1698-1749). Continuing the family tradition (and making life very difficult for genealogists), his eldest son was also named Joseph (1729-1789) and all were farmers at Stubbing. As 'stubbin' simply meant land cleared of trees (stubs being stumps), there would have been numerous sites with the name in the locality but the best-known remains that off Dobroyd Hill. Our latest Joseph married Sarah Battye (Batty) around 1760, and a document has survived which records his duty to do so:

> *Know all by me these presents, that we Joseph Gaunt of Upper Denby*
> *in the Parish of Penistone in the County of York, Cordwainer and*
> *Martin Batty of Upper Denby in the Parish and County aforesaid,*
> *Clothier are bound.*

This was an obligation document, signed by both father and prospective son-in-law, that Joseph would marry Sarah and there was no let or hindrance. The surety was £200, to be paid by Joseph if the marriage did not take place. A cordwainer (in British tradition) was a shoemaker who made new shoes from new leather, as opposed to a cobbler who simply mended old shoes, though today the term cobbler describes both occupations. A clothier from around this time made his living from supplying wool, usually to women who would spin it on a wheel in front of the hearth, and yarn to the men, who would weave it using a loom usually in the upper storeys of the house. Many upper floors were fitted with extra windows in order to improve the light for this operation. For the male weavers, this was often a second income that would supplement a day's wage employed in agriculture, for instance. Once the spinning and weaving were completed, the clothier would collect the pieces and pay a wage dependent upon the number of pieces they had produced (hence the term piece-work). He would then arrange for them to be sold on to be used by tailors and other cloth workers. By the mid-eighteenth century, it was not unusual for the clothier to own the looms and rent them to the weavers, deducting a rental charge for the machine from their wages.

Thankfully, the marriage took place, thereby saving Joseph a vast sum that in today's money would be well over £28,000 and possibly much more. Unsurprisingly they christened their eldest son Joseph (1760-1850). The following is a transcription of Joseph's last will:

Last Will and Testament of Joseph Gaunt of Upper Denby 1789.
In the name of God Amen. I Joseph Gaunt of Denby in the parish of
Penistone in the County of York, Yeoman, do this 5th day of August in the
year of our Lord one thousand seven hundred and eighty nine make and
publish this my last will and testament in manner and form following.

First I give, devise and bequeath unto my son Joseph Gaunt all that freehold estate situate at Stubbing in the Township of Denby aforesaid and in the possession of my said son, Joseph together with all the appurtenances thereunto belonging to have and to hold to him the said Joseph Gaunt, his heirs and assigns forever, charged and chargeable with the following legacies, sums and payments (to wit) that from the time of my decease till all my children shall attain the age of twenty one years, he shall pay to my executors hereinafter mentioned the sum of sixteen pounds yearly to be paid by two equal half yearly payments at Whitsuntide and Martinmas and to be applied by them as hereinto after directed and as soon as all my children shall have attained the age of twenty one years then that my said son, Joseph Gaunt shall pay to my daughter Elizabeth Chadwick, my son William Gaunt, my son Jonathan Gaunt, my daughter Bridget Gaunt, my son, James Gaunt, my daughter, Mary Gaunt, my son, Thomas Gaunt, my son, John Gaunt and my daughter, Ann Gaunt the sum of three hundred and fifty pounds to be equally divided amongst them, share and share alike, and also that my said son, Joseph Gaunt, at the decease of my wife, shall pay the further sum of two hundred pounds to be equally divided amongst my nine sons and daughters above named, share and share alike. But in case any of my children shall before any or all the above legacies become due and so dying leaves no heir then the legacy or legacies that would have become due to such child or children to be paid to my executors and to be applied by them as hereunto directed. Also I give and bequeath with the consent of William Bosville Esq. my landlord and of Miss Walker, my landlady, to my wife, Sarah Gaunt the tenant right of my farm at Denby and the tenant right of two closes of land belonging to Miss Walker she giving her promissory note bearing interest to my executors for the tillage in the land and corn sown to be valued according to the custom of the County and at the decease of my said wife or upon her marriage or when she shall choose to give up the said farm and closes of land, it is my will with the consent of my landlord and landlady aforesaid that my two sons, Jonathan and James do succeed her in the said farm and closes of land, they paying for the tillage and crops as aforesaid. And in case my wife shall choose to give up the said farm and closes of land to my said sons, Jonathan and James during her widowhood I then give and bequeath to my said wife one house situate in Denby aforesaid now in the occupation of John Wordsworth for and during the term of her natural life and also such part of my household furniture as she shall choose, not amounting in the whole to more than the value of ten pounds.

And I give and bequeath all the rest, residue and remainder of my estate and effects whatsoever to Mr Nathaniel Shirt of Denby Mill, my son Joseph Gaunt and John Chadwick of Batley in the County aforesaid, upon trust and to and for the uses, intents and purposes hereinafter declared, that is to say, upon trust, that first they pay all my lawful debts and funeral expenses and whereas my son, Joseph, my daughter, Elizabeth, my son, William and my son, Jonathan have been advanced cash of them in the sum of twenty pounds during my life, that they, my executors do pay to such of my other children as may have attained twenty one years of age, the like sum of twenty pounds, six months after my decease and also to such others of my children as may be under twenty one years of age at my decease the like sum of twenty pounds when they attain the age of twenty one respectively, and also that my executors apply so much of my personal estate as they may think proper to the maintenance and education of such of my children as may be underage at my decease. And the surplus of my personal estate with the sixteen pounds payable yearly to my executor out of my real estate and also any legacy or legacies that may have come to my executors in consequence of the death of any of my children to be divided equally amongst all my surviving children, share and share alike as soon as my youngest child shall attain the age of twenty one. But in case any of my children shall die before all or any of the above heirs legacies are due to them and so dying leave their respective legacies to go to their heirs.

And I do hereby appoint the said Mr Nathaniel Shirt, my said son, Joseph Gaunt and the said John Chadwick and the survivor or survivors of them executors of this my last will and testament whom I do authorise to deduct out of my personal estate all reasonable charges and expenses they may be at, in and about the execution of the said will and testament. In witness whereof I have to this, my last will and testament set my hand and seal the day and year first above written.

Signed, sealed, published and declared by the said testator as and for this last will and testament in the presence of us:
John Hardy, Joshua Gaunt, Jonathan Firth.

NB: Jonathan Firth signed with a cross by his name.

An inventory of goods and chattels taken this 14th of November 1789 belonging Joseph Gaunt of Denby in the parish of Penistone deceased by Jonathan Wood and Daniel Dyson.

	£	s	d
Purse and Apparel	*5*	*0*	*0*
Household Furniture	*41*	*13*	*5*
Live Stock	*21*	*0*	*7*
Hay and Corn	*20*	*0*	*0*
TOTAL	*87*	*14*	*0*

Returning to our latest Joseph Gaunt (1760–1850), he married Hannah English, possibly at Denby, if not then at Penistone. The service was conducted by the Denby assistant curate Jeremiah Bourn in 1787, both husband and wife signed their own names proving they were literate. Although Joseph was originally of Stubbing (where he was also noted to be operating as a worsted manufacturer), he removed to Denby Hall (farm) prior to 1841. The hall had been let to tenant farmers since it was sold by the old Burdet lords of Denby to the Saviles of Thornhill by 1643. Originally, the Burdets rented it back, but as money had dwindled due to family disputes, they eventually abandoned it. We can also find Joseph in the Yorkshire Poll of 5 May 1807, when he voted for Viscount Milton. In the 1841 census, we can find an aged Joseph (now 80) living with two of his sons, John and Robert (all denoted as farmers), plus John's three children, William, Hugh and Hannah, and two servants. Hannah had died two years before the survey took place and was buried at Denby by Brive Bronwin. Joseph finally died in 1850, the year before the next census was taken.

Last Will and Testament of Joseph Gaunt of Upper Denby 1847.

I Joseph Gaunt of Upper Denby in the Parish of Penistone in the West Riding of the County of York, Yeoman, being of sound mind, memory and understanding, do for the settling of my worldly affairs make and declare this my last will and testament in manner and form following (that is to say). First – I will, order and direct that all my just debts, financial and testamentary charges and expenses be duly paid and discharged out of my Personal Estate and effects by my executor hereinafter named. I hereby nominate, constitute and appoint my son, John Gaunt and my son in law Richard Jackson, then their heirs, executors or administrators joint executors of this my last will and testament. To whom I give devise and bequeath all my real estate situate and being at Stubbing within the Township of Denby aforesaid. Also two cottages or dwelling houses situate and being at Upper Denby aforesaid together with all and singular my monies, securities for money, book debts, furniture, goods, chattels and effects whatsoever or whatsoever the sum may be which I may be possessed of at my decease.

Nevertheless in trust for the hereinafter mentioned purposes I give, devise and bequeath unto my son, John Gaunt, his heirs and assigns all my real estate and being at Stubbing on the Township of Denby aforesaid and now in the occupation of James Peace or his undertenants. Also two cottages or dwelling houses with their gardens and appurtenances thereto, belonging, situate and being at Upper Denby and called or known by the name of Ratten Row, also the tenant right and interest in the land I hold and retain under William Smith Esquire, together with all my monies, securities for money, book debts, furniture, goods, chattels and effects whatsoever which I may be possessed of at my decease.

Nevertheless, subject to the hereinafter mentioned legacies, annuities and bequests. Viz: I give and bequest unto my Grandchildren, the children of my own daughter Elizabeth (deceased) to them their heirs or assigns four hundred pounds of lawful money current in Great Britain to be equally divided amongst them, share and share alike to be paid them within twelve calendar months next after my decease. I also give and bequeath unto my daughter Martha, the wife of James Brown an annuity of sixteen pounds a year, yearly and every year during her material life to be paid in by quarterly instalments such annuity to commence after my decease and at the decease of my aforesaid daughter Martha then I give and bequeath unto her children their heirs or assigns or the executors of their heirs or assigns four hundred pounds of money current in Great Britain to be equally divided amongst them, share and share alike to be paid therein within twelve calendar months next after my decease. I also give and bequeath unto my son Robert Gaunt an annuity of sixteen pounds a year, yearly and every year during his natural life to be paid him every month or oftener if required and to commence immediately after my decease. Also I give and bequeath unto my son, Matthias Gaunt, now in Van Diemen's Land, his heirs or assigns three hundred pounds of lawful money current in Great Britain to be paid him within twelve calendar months next after my decease. Further, my will is that my said executors shall reimburse themselves all reasonable costs and charges they lay out or be paid unto in or about the trusts in them reposed and that they shall not be answerable or accountable of my effects than shall actually come into their hands. Neither shall one of their heirs, executors or administrators be answerable or accountable for the other of their acts, deeds or defaults. And lastly I do hereby revoke all former wills, legacies and bequests by me at any time hereforeto and do declare this to be my last will and testament.

In witness I the said testator Joseph Gaunt have to this my last will and testament set my hand and at this twenty eight day of June in the Year of our Lord one thousand eight hundred and forty seven.

Signed, sealed, published and declared by the said testator, Joseph Gaunt as said for his last will and testament in the presence of us at his request and in the presence of each other have subscribed our names as witnesses attesting the due execution hereof.

Signed by: Joseph Gaunt, Joshua Gaunt, John Hinchcliff and William Thorp.

In the 1851 census returns we can still find John, by now, head of the household and described as a farmer of 60 acres and employing one man, but of course he had his own family to help out with all the agricultural activities. All except one.

John Gaunt's younger son Matthias was born three years later than John in 1793. Little is known about Matthias's early life. No doubt he initially lent a hand on the family farm but his life altered greatly when an inherent wanderlust took over and he decided to join the Royal Navy as a ship's doctor or surgeon. The Company of Barber-Surgeons had been undertaking the training and examination of ship's surgeons since 1626, but though the company had been phased out by the time of Matthias, they still carried out examinations. During the Age of Sail (roughly the sixteenth century through to the mid-nineteenth), the Royal Navy carried medical officers on board all of its warships. These surgeons were not required to have a medical degree and were generally trained by apprenticeship. Surgeons were assisted by surgeon's mates and they were then, in turn, assisted by boys, known as loblolly boys, named after a gruel usually served in the sick-bay.

It is currently unknown as to where and with whom Matthias undertook his apprenticeship though the city of Edinburgh has passed down orally through the family. His sword has survived with his Australian descendants through to the present day, it was probably largely ceremonial but also a useful weapon in times of peril.

A surgeon in the navy at this time was not necessarily well-paid and they were obliged to supply themselves with a full medical kit consisting of instruments that were capable of amputation, trephining (brain and skull operations), bleeding and cupping, probing and draining, and dentistry, amongst other things. These instruments would now look to be very much at home in a chamber of horrors. A set of instruments could cost between eighteen and twenty-five guineas (well over £1,000 in 2016) and the average pay for the surgeon was from around five to fourteen pounds a month (£5 = around £311, and £14 = around £900, in 2016). Far from being sufficient to provide instruments and medicines for an entire crew on a long sea voyage, the surgeon would amass his instruments as cheaply as possible, the quality of which would vary along with the manufacturer. His length of service in the Navy or any conflicts he was involved in is currently unknown, but family tradition suggests he did travel to South America, he may also have been involved in the British struggle to stop the slave trade after it was abolished in 1807.

By the time Matthias had reached his early thirties, he had left the navy and had begun practising as a surgeon at Cripplegate in London, he had set up in business by 1825 and was still operating in 1830. Some time prior to 1825 Matthias had met Frances Green, and in that year had married her at Essendon near Hatfield, Hertfordshire. Frances (born 25 April 1804) was the daughter of Isaac and Frances Green and the sister of Richard. Two of their children were christened at St Giles, Cripplegate: Sydney (1826) and Frances (1828), when Matthias was described as a surgeon of Castle Street. This may have been his own practice or a partnership, but it is also possible, considering his background that he had connections to the Greenwich naval base, which was only 5½ miles away, the hospital here did not close down until 1869. A further child, Jane, was added to the family before Matthias made the decision to emigrate to Australia in 1829.

Why would Matthias have made the decision to uproot his family, endure an eight-month journey at sea and leave behind them all that was familiar? As a member of the British Empire, it was required that the first colonists become self-sufficient. The distance and time involved meant aid from home was not a possibility. The convicts were used to supply labour for the colonists, but the vast majority had no experience of agriculture, particularly in a country so different to their own. With the colony facing starvation and death, the New South Wales governor persuaded the British government to send more farmers with the promise of land grants, labour and servants, but they were still vastly outnumbered by the convicts. By 1800, the immediate risks to the colony had reduced, although skilled labourers were still thin on the ground. The assisted passage scheme was begun in 1830. This required the purchase of colonial land, the proceeds of which were used to pay for poorer migrants to emigrate, and during the next twenty years, around 187,000 free settlers arrived in Australia. Many of the migrants were victims of the Industrial Revolution, which decreased the home market for manual labour and left many in workhouses or slums and for whom the opportunity for a new life became appealing. Over time, the free settlers gradually came to outnumber the convicts, who had either been pardoned or released on completion of their sentences. It must also be stated that Matthias took advantage of buying the land because of 'the severity of the English climate'.

The destination chosen by Matthias was Tasmania, or Van Diemen's Land, and he and his young family boarded the ship *Eliza* as free settlers in August 1830. Matthias and Frances's son, Matthias junior, was born on 9 August 1830, and as such a young baby would have placed incredible pressure and responsibility upon Frances. Matthias was on his way to buy colonial land on which to bring up his family. During the journey, he was responsible for performing a burial at sea and taking prayers – presumably on a Sunday. It was also during the voyage that he acquired eleven merino sheep in Capetown, South Africa, to bring to Tasmania with him.

The ship's Captain Weddelland landed in Hobart on 1 May 1831, and Matthias and his family, including 9-month-old baby Matthias junior, had made the journey successfully with Matthias is possession of letters of recommendation to the governor of the colonies. Matthias shortly applied for and was granted land on the east bank of the River Tamar, about 15 miles from Launceston, and he immediately began to clear it and improve it (utilising his convict labourers) and naming his new home after the Lake District village of Windermere. He was not alone, as the number of free settlers buying land rapidly increased at this time, many picking out the best farming areas between Launceston and Hobart Town, just as he had done. Matthias built a saw mill at Windermere, though later he converted it to a steam-powered flour mill. He also established a vineyard and produced wine. He did not practise as a surgeon in Tasmania though he could be induced to render aid if necessary and give consultations. He donated land to and largely paid for the erection of an Anglican church dedicated, not unnaturally, to St Matthias, on the bank of the Tamar river. He became a magistrate and held various directorships such as at the Commercial Bank in Launceston, the Cornwall Fire & Marine Insurance Company and the Launceston Bank Company, he was also politically active.

Matthias became part of the anti-transportation league movement, though despite this he did have the luxury of free labour courtesy of the convicts when he first arrived, something which continued for a further twenty years. He can be found complaining about the convicts of Norfolk Island being 'sent down like a pestilence' upon Van Diemen's Land. The movement was established to oppose penal transportation to Australia and began in Tasmania in the late 1840s. The onset of the Victorian gold rush in 1851 led the British government to abolish transportation as it was seen as an incentive for criminal activity in order to be taken to Eastern Australia. The last convict ship to be sent from England to Australia arrived in 1853, and the need for the anti-transportation league was now defunct.

Matthias eventually left the running of Windermere to his sons and moved into Launceston with Frances in around 1853. They had continued to add to their family after their arrival in Tasmania. Their fifth child was named Joseph Stubbing Gaunt, a reference and acknowledgement to Matthias's father's place of occupation and work and indeed that of the families for hundreds of years. John, Thomas, Emma, Edward, Richard Francis, Elizabeth Coppack, William, Charles, Ellen and James were all to follow, making a family of fifteen children in all, though there were tragedies long the way. William died after just eight days, Matthias junior aged 13, Thomas aged 20, and Emma aged 19. The year 1854 was particularly harsh on the family, John was drowned, Ellen died of tonsillitis and James of inflammation.

Edward became a stockbroker and had interests in numerous mines around Tasmania, he became well-known as a mine manager. But life was not always easy and he spent much of it in and out of bankruptcy, though when he died his death was widely reported throughout Australia. His brother Charles was also a little imprudent with money and spent sixteen months in prison for embezzlement.

Matthias died in 1874 in Launceston and, as a mark of respect, the ships in the harbour lowered their flags to half-mast and many of the shops and business partially closed their shutters to mark his passing – he made his final journey back home to Windermere to be buried by his family. Frances died six years later in 1880. The farmer's boy from Denby had made rather a success of his new life down under and he is fondly remembered by his many descendants still living there today.

Matthias Gaunt, 1794-1874.

Frances Gaunt, nee Green, wife of Matthias.

Richard Green, brother of Frances Green.

A letter of application for land for Matthias Gaunt, dated May 1831.

Nº 2.

May 4th 18 31

Sir,

I request that you will be pleased to submit to His Excellency The Governor, through the proper Channel, this my Application for a Grant of Land.

I have to state, for His Excellency's Information, that I arrived in the Colony in the Year *P.S.!* that I am a Native of *Yorkshire England* that my Age is *30* years, and that I am possessed of Capital to the Amount of £ *2 3 15 1 1* Sterling, as specified on the other side, all of which I intend to devote to Agricultural Pursuits in this Colony ; and, in order to afford satisfactory Proof, with respect to Character, and that I am really possessed of Capital to the foregoing Amount, I beg leave to refer to

[The Certificate or Certificates and other Documents, as the case may be).

herewith transmitted.

I have the honor to be,

Sir,

Your most obedient humble Servant;

Matthias Gaunt

on board the Eliza

To GEORGE FRANKLAND, Esq.
Surveyor General, &c. &c. &c.
Hobarton.

The pommel of Matthias Gaunt's sabre.

A detail of the hilt and blade of Matthias Gaunt's sabre.

Detail of the guard of Matthias Gaunt's sabre.

Matthias Gaunt's music organ, now on display at Entally House, Hadspen, which is a fifteen-minute drive from Launceston, Tasmania.

From right to left, a photograph of Frances Green, Matthias Gaunt's medicine scales and a medal awarded to Matthias for his work in support of the Anti-Transportation League.

74   Matthias Gaunt's flute.

St Matthias Anglican Church, Windermere. When Matthias Gaunt decided to emigrate to Australia, his wife was concerned that there might not be a church wherever they ended up settling. He promised Frances that if there wasn't he would build one for her. True to his word, it was consecrated in 1845 and has now become one of Australia's oldest churches to be in continuous use since its foundation.

The grave of Matthias Gaunt (and two of his children) situated at the church he was responsible for founding.

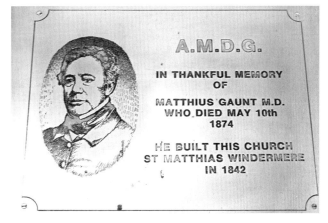

A plaque on the interior wall of St Matthias church in commemoration of Matthias Gaunt.

75

Fig 1 – Descent from Robert Gaunt, born 1635

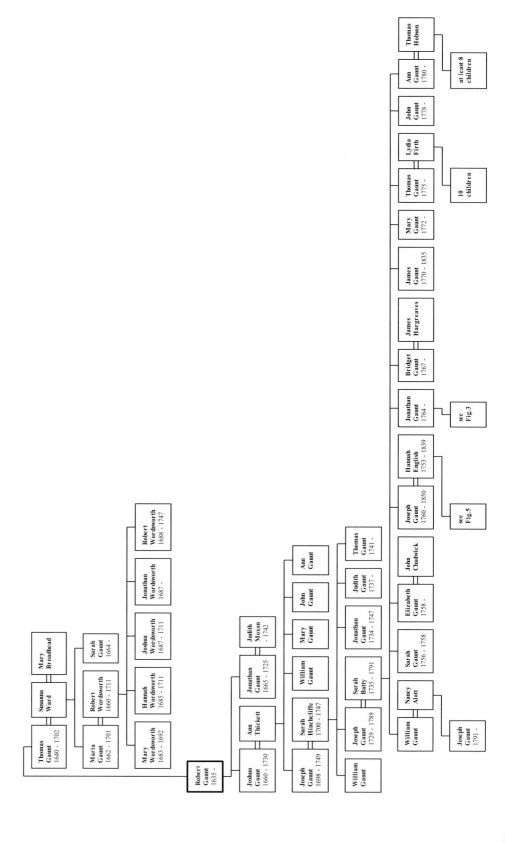

Fig 2 – Descent from Jonathan Gaunt, 1665-1725

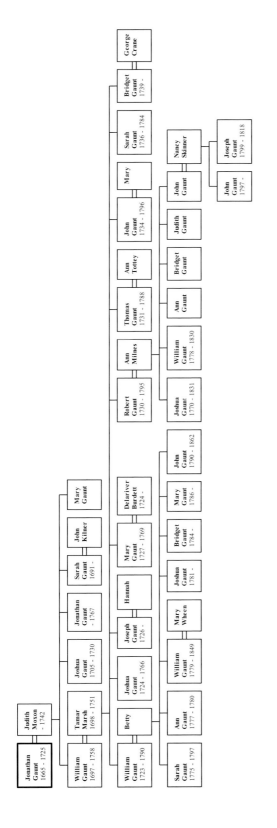

Fig 3 – Descent from Jonathan Gaunt, 1764-unknown

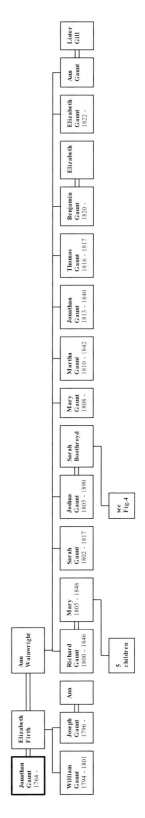

Fig 4 – Descent from Joshua Gaunt, 1805-1890

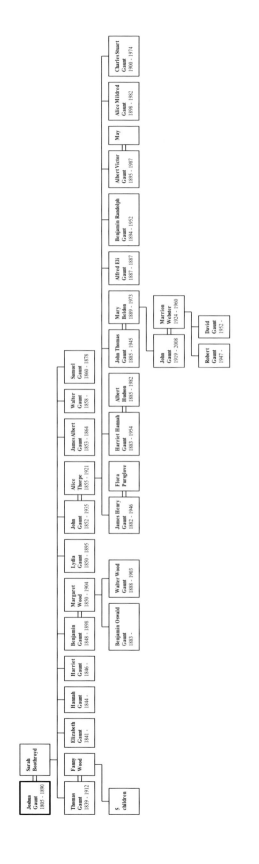

Fig 5 – Matthias Gaunt immediate family

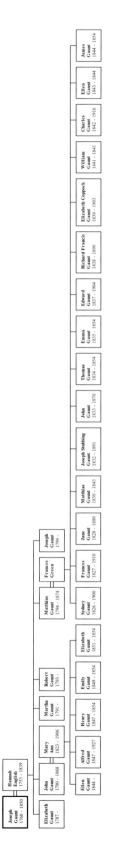

𝕌pper 𝔇enby and 𝔇enby 𝔇ale 𝔅rass 𝔅ands

**Upper Denby Brass Band – formed 1922 – disbanded around 1960
(The Denby United Silver Prize Brass Band)**

The following is an incomplete list of the competitions that the band played in, their final position and the conductor if known.

Date	Competition Name & Venue	Pos.	Conductor
29 September 1923	Crystal Palace (Junior Shield – B)		J W Garratt
7 May 1927	Belle Vue Contest		
7 September 1929	Huddersfield & District BBA Contest (Section B)		
5 September 1931	Huddersfield & District BBA Contest (Section A)		
5 September 1931	Huddersfield & District BBA Contest (Section B)		
3 September 1932	Huddersfield & District BBA Contest (Section A)	2nd	
6 May 1933	Belle Vue May Contest (Class B Group 2)		Willie Kaye
9 September 1933	Butlin's Holiday Camp Contest		
13 August 1938	Rotherham Contest		
10 May 1947	Belle Vue May Contest (Class D Section 2)		S Woodcock
8 May 1948	Belle Vue May Contest (Class C Group 2)		S Woodcock
19 March 1949	North East Area (Third Section)		Willie Kaye
7 May 1949	Belle Vue May Contest (Class C)		Willie Kaye
27 May 1950	Belle Vue May Contest (Class D)	1st	Jack Fisher
2 September 1950	Huddersfield & District BBA Contest (Section B)	4th	
26 May 1951	Belle Vue May Contest (Class C)		Jack Bacon
15 March 1952	North Eastern Area (Fourth Section)	6th	Jack Bacon
17 May 1952	Spring Festival – Junior Cup		Jack Bacon

Denby Dale Brass Band 1872-1966

The following is an extensive though incomplete list of the competitions that the band played in, their final position and conductor if known.

Date	Competition Name & Venue	Pos.	Conductor
13 July 1872	Shelley Contest		J Hirst
16 August 1873	Kirkburton Contest		
30 May 1874	Marsh Contest		John Berry
19 September 1874	Honley Contest		John Berry
14 August 1875	Stalybridge Contest	2	
3 June 1876	Golcar Contest		
17 June 1876	Huddersfield Contest		John Berry
1 July 1876	Greenfield Contest	1	
1 July 1876	Saltaire	5	A Hanwell
12 August 1876	Shepley Own Choice Contest	3	John Berry
21 August 1876	Grenoside Contest	2	John Berry
30 June 1877	Huddersfield Contest		Edwin Swift
25 June 1881	Thurlstone Contest		
23 June 1883	Gorton Contest	1	B Stead
28 June 1884	Thurlstone Contest		R Stead
26 July 1884	Lindley Contest	3	R Stead
16 August 1884	Wyke	4	R Stead
16 August 1884	Sheepridge	3	R Stead
23 August 1884	Barnsley Contest	5	
6 September 1884	Staveley Contest	1	R Stead
8 September 1884	Worsborough Dale Contest	4	R Stead
27 September 1884	Leeds Contest	3	R Stead
29 November 1884	Derby Contest	4	John Gladney Jnr.
30 June 1885	Boston Contest		
1 August 1885	Huddersfield Belle Vue Gardens Contest	1	
29 August 1885	Chapeltown Contest	3	
21 May 1887	Copley Contest	6	Fenton Renshaw
25 June 1887	Thurlstone Contest		
19 September 1887	Hoyland Contest	4	Fenton Renshaw

21 May 1888	Holmfirth Contest	2	
21 July 1888	Holmfirth Contest	2	Fenton Renshaw
4 May 1889	Wyke Contest	3	
11 May 1889	Elland Contest		Fenton Renshaw
8 June 1889	Great Horton Contest	4	
10 June 1889	Holmfirth March Contest	2	
27 July 1889	Morley Contest		
17 August 1889	Chapeltown Contest	1	
26 May 1890	Holmfirth March Contest	1	
14 June 1890	Rotherham Contest	4	
9 May 1891	Shelley Contest	3	
18 May 1891	Holmfirth Contest	1	
19 May 1891	Huddersfield Band of Hope Union Conts.		
15 August 1891	Woodhouse Contest	2	Fenton Renshaw
13 May 1893	Bradford Contest	3	
19 August 1893	Woodhouse Contest	4	Fenton Renshaw
19 August 1893	Penistone Contest	4	Fenton Renshaw
12 May 1894	Skelmanthorpe Contest	4	Fenton Renshaw
14 May 1894	Holmfirth March Contest	1	Fenton Renshaw
14 July 1894	Rotherham Contest	1	Fenton Renshaw
18 August 1894	Woodhouse Contest	1	Fenton Renshaw
25 August 1894	Gainsborough Contest	1	
25 August 1894	Crigglestone Contest	1	Fenton Renshaw
8 September 1894	Clayton West Contest	2	Fenton Renshaw
15 September 1894	Keighley Contest	4	Fenton Renshaw
1 June 1895	Holmfirth Contest	1	Fenton Renshaw

14 December 1895	Sheffield Contest	3	Fenton Renshaw
6 April 1896	Elsecar Contest	1	Fenton Renshaw
11 April 1896	Rotherham Contest		
9 May 1896	Skelmanthorpe Contest	1	Fenton Renshaw
16 May 1896	Rotherham Contest	3	Fenton Renshaw
25 May 1896	Holmfirth Contest	1	
20 June 1896	Wharncliffe Silkstone Contest	4	Fenton Renshaw
25 July 1896	Shepley Own Choice Contest		Fenton Renshaw
25 July 1896	Shepley March Contest		Fenton Renshaw
15 August 1896	Handsworth Woodhouse Contest	1	Fenton Renshaw
22 August 1896	Gainsborough Contest	1	
19 April 1897	Elsecar Contest	4	
7 June 1897	Holmfirth March Contest	1	Fenton Renshaw
19 August 1899	Kirkcaldy Contest		
7 October 1899	Holmfirth Contest	3	Fenton Renshaw
22 June 1903	Castleford Contest	9	
26 September 1903	Great Britain National Finals – Crystal Palace – Fourth Section		Fenton Renshaw
20 July 1907	Clayton West Contest	2	Fenton Renshaw
17 August 1907	Silkstone Contest	4	Fenton Renshaw
29 May 1909	Normanton Contest		
19 June 1909	Thorne Contest		
26 June 1909	Skelmanthorpe Contest	3	Tom Eastwood
7 February 1914	Clayton (Bradford) Contest		Tom Eastwood
13 August 1921	Nortonthorpe Own Choice Contest	3	William Heap

Date	Event		Conductor
29 September 1923	Great Britain National Finals – Crystal Palace – Junior Cup B		Joseph Crawford Dyson
27 September 1924	Great Britain National Finals – Crystal Palace – Junior Cup B		Joseph Crawford Dyson
26 September 1925	Great Britain National Finals – Crystal Palace – Junior Shield A		Joseph Crawford Dyson
25 September 1926	Great Britain National Finals – Crystal Palace – Junior Shield A		Joseph Crawford Dyson
7 May 1927	Crow Edge Contest		
28 May 1927	Renishaw Contest	2	Joseph Crawford Dyson
18 June 1927	Sheffield Hospitals Contest – Senior Cup	3	Joseph Crawford Dyson
18 June 1927	Sheffield Hospitals Contest – Junior Cup	1	Joseph Crawford Dyson
24 September 1927	Great Britain National Finals – Crystal Palace – Junior Shield B	7	Joseph Crawford Dyson
30 June 1928	Grimethorpe Contest		
28 July 1928	Sheffield Contest		
7 September 1929	Huddersfield & District BBA (Section A)		
27 September 1930	Great Britain National Finals – Crystal Palace – Junior Shield A	3	Noel Thorpe
5 September 1931	Huddersfield & District BBA (Section A)	1	Noel Thorpe
5 September 1931	Huddersfield & District BBA (Section B)	1	Noel Thorpe
1 October 1932	Great Britain National Finals – Crystal Palace – Junior Cup B		Noel Thorpe
2 September 1933	Huddersfield & District BBA (Section A)		
5 May 1934	Belle Vue May Contest (Class A)	2	Noel Thorpe
14 July 1934	Belle Vue July Contest (Class B)		
4 May 1935	Belle Vue May Contest (Class A)	1	Noel Thorpe
29 June 1935	Flockton Contest	3	Noel Thorpe

11 July 1936	Belle Vue July Contest		
1 May 1937	Holme Valley Brass Band Contest (Section A)	4	Noel Thorpe
26 June 1937	Flockton Contest	1	Noel Thorpe
10 July 1937	Belle Vue July Contest	4	Noel Thorpe
28 August 1937	Haworth Contest	1	Noel Thorpe
4 September 1937	Huddersfield & District BBA (Section A)	1	Noel Thorpe
23 October 1937	Wakefield Contest	2	Noel Thorpe
5 March 1938	City of Leicester Brass Band Festival (Championship Section)		
21 May 1938	Holme Valley Brass Band Contest (Section A)	4	Noel Thorpe
2 July 1938	Huddersfield Carnival Contest	1	Noel Thorpe
9 July 1938	Belle Vue July Contest (Class A)		Noel Thorpe
27 August 1938	Haworth Contest	3	Noel Thorpe
12 November 1938	Wakefield Contest	1	Noel Thorpe
25 March 1939	Sale (Lido) Contest		
13 May 1939	Holme Valley Brass Band Contest (Section A)		
8 July 1939	Belle Vue July Contest		Noel Thorpe
2 September 1939	Huddersfield & District BBA (Section A)	1	
27 April 1940	Holme Valley Brass Band Contest (Section A)		
31 August 1940	Huddersfield & District BBA (Section A)	3	Noel Thorpe
26 August 1944	Huddersfield & District BBA (Section A)	2	Noel Thorpe
31 August 1946	Huddersfield & District BBA (Section B)	2	Noel Thorpe
26 May 1951	Belle Vue May Contest (Class D)		J E Pearson
18 April 1953	Great Britain National Contest – North Eastern Area (Third Section) Bradford		H Ryder
27 June 1953	Bradford Contest	3	H Ryder
13 March 1954	Great Britain National Contest – North East Area (Fourth Section) Bradford		E Wilkinson
22 May 1954	Spring Festival – British Open & Qualifying (Junior Trophy)		E Wilkinson
4 September 1954	Huddersfield & District BBA (Section B)	3	
4 December 1955	Huddersfield & District BBA (Section B)	4	
14 April 1956	Great Britain National Contest – North Eastern Area (Fourth Section) Bradford		Noel Thorpe
27 October 1956	National Championship of Great Britain (Fourth Section Final) Shepherds Bush, London.		

Date	Contest		
25 November 1956	Yorkshire Invitation Contest – Huddersfield		
6 April 1957	Great Britain National Contest – North Eastern Area (Third Section) Bradford		Noel Thorpe
18 May 1957	British Open & Qualifying – Senior Trophy – Belle Vue, Manchester		Noel Thorpe
1 March 1958	Great Britain National Contest – North Eastern Area – (Fourth Section) Bradford	1	Noel Thorpe
25 October 1958	National Championship of Great Britain (Fourth Section Final) Hammersmith, London		K Blackwood
14 March 1959	Great Britain National Contest – North East Area – (Third Section) Bradford	4	Jack Fisher
9 May 1959	British Open & Qualifying – Senior Trophy – Belle Vue, Manchester		F C Fisher
28 June 1959	Yorkshire Transport Contest	4	Jack Fisher
6 September 1959	Huddersfield & District BBA (Section A)	2	
6 December 1959	Huddersfield & District BBA (Section A)	5	Jack Fisher
6 March 1960	CISWO Yorkshire (2nd Section)	5	Jack Fisher
2 April 1960	Great Britain Area Contests – North Eastern Area (Third Section)		Jack Fisher
28 May 1960	British Open & Qualifying – Senior Trophy		Jack Fisher
8 October 1960	Bury Contest	3	Jack Fisher
23 October 1960	Yorkshire Transport Contest	3	
19 November 1960	Wigan Contest	2	Jack Fisher
5 March 1961	CISWO Yorkshire (3rd Section)	1	Jack Fisher
25 March 1961	Great Britain Area Contests – North Eastern Area (Third Section)		Jack Fisher
6 May 1961	Holme Valley Brass Band Contest Section A		Jack Fisher
14 October 1961	Bury Contest	5	Jack Fisher
4 November 1961	Wigan Contest	1	
19 November 1961	Horbury Victoria Prize Band Brass Band Contest	1	
4 March 1962	CISWO Yorkshire (2nd Section)		Jack Fisher
14 March 1964	Great Britain Area Contests – North Eastern Area – Second Section		Eric Foster
27 June 1964	Yorkshire Brass Bands Summer Festival (Class A)	2	Eric Foster

6 March 1965	Great Britain Area Contests – North Eastern Area – Second Section		Eric Foster
6 March 1966	CISWO Yorkshire (2nd Section)		Eric Crossley
12 March 1966	Great Britain National Contest – Yorkshire Brass Band Championships – Second Section	1	

NB: CISWO = Coal Industry Social Welfare Organisation.

Denby Dale Brass Band were, at times, no strangers to success. Competition victories were achieved by four notable conductors:

Fenton Renshaw
Fenton was born in 1852 to William and Sarah Renshaw of Brockholes. He married Elizabeth Boothroyd of Farnley Tyas and began a family. In 1881, his day job was that of a woollen spinner in a mill, but his passion for brass bands began with learning to play the euphonium. He had become a conductor by at least 1876, and continued until his death in 1909. He had been mentored by John Gladney (1839-1911), who was one of the giants in the world of brass bands. His work with Denby Dale began in 1887 (it could have been a little earlier), and his last mention was in 1907. He began his musical career in his home town of Honley, from 1876 until 1885, but after this he began to range further afield. He was conducting in places such as Rotherham, Rawmarsh, Leek, Doncaster, Peterborough, Lincoln, Scunthorpe and many others, though he did keep returning to Honley and Denby Dale. Fenton became one of the more successful band trainers of the 1880s and 1890s, and was the professional conductor to over fifty bands. His death at the comparatively early age of 57 took place before he could reach full maturity as a conductor, yet his success spoke for itself. Evidently, Gladney had passed on some of his skills.

Joseph Crawford Dyson
Joseph was born in 1883 in Dewsbury, one of at least eight children to his parents William H and Emma. In 1901, he can be found living with his parents in Gomersal and working as a small wiredrawer, but he was almost certainly involved with brass bands by this time as only five years later he was conducting Cleckheaton Temperance Band. He married Lily Newsome in 1921 just prior to becoming involved with the Denby Dale Band from 1923 to around 1927. He was a notable cornet player but became a conductor, band trainer and adjudicator. He left Yorkshire during the late 1920s and moved to

Joseph Crawford Dyson 1883-1945 – Denby Dale band master.

86

Greater London. As with his predecessor, he led many different bands over the years including Hanwell Silver, Horsham Borough, Grays, Enfield, Northfleet (and while still in Yorkshire, the Brighouse and Rastrick), and many others, and continued to do so until his death was recorded in Brentford in 1945.

Noel Thorpe
Noel (born in 1889) was involved with Denby Dale Band from 1930 up until 1958 and led them to numerous competition victories. His career began in 1911 with Horbury Band, but as with the previous two conductors, he did not limit himself to one village or town. Throughout his career, he led numerous different bands, including Slaithwaite, Blackhall Colliery, Carlton Main, Flockton United, Heworth Colliery and even the brass band of the Rowntree's Cocoa Works in York. He was described as 'respected but much feared', and that he had 'an autocratic teaching style'. Noel died in 1970 aged 81.

Jack Fisher
Jack commenced his conducting career with the Upper Denby Silver Prize Band in 1950, although he had moved on to Skelmanthorpe by 1952. From 1953 to 1955 he was with the Thurlstone Band before taking over at Denby Dale in 1959. He remained here until 1962 and oversaw some excellent competition results. He was back at Skelmanthorpe in 1964 and re-joined Thurlstone in 1965, before making the move to Hade Edge Band in 1969, where he remained until 1984. Whilst here, Jack had many successes, which also included winning BBC Radio Sheffield's 'Bold as Brass' contest in 1982 and 1983 (Hade Edge were the runners up in 1984). He also hosted a request programme on the same station. His final move was to Meltham & Meltham Mills in 1985 until 1989. He died in 1990.

Denby United Silver Prize Band at an unknown competition. Circa 1930.   87

A newspaper cutting from the Manchester edition of the *Daily Herald* dated 11 July 1938. The caption reads: In step, in time and in tune, Denby Dale bandsmen march past judges, audience and make believe scenery at Belle Vue, Manchester, on Saturday. They were competing in the 53rd Annual July Brass Band Contest, the chief event of which was won by the newly formed Fairey Aviation Company Limited.

The Denby Dale Junior Brass Band, taken around the 1930s.

The Turton Family – The Denby Doctors

We have examined this family of Denby doctors before across the Denby & District series of books, but research always brings to light new stories and the present day members of the family continue to share their discoveries with me and also some very old photographs.

Thomas Turton (1846-about 1938) was the son of Thomas Turton and Betty Rhodes of Denby and the grandson of Thomas Turton and Amelia Ward. And he resided at Pinfold House. All three men were surgeons and apothecaries. Thomas, born in 1846, became a qualified doctor in Manchester before he married Ann Hargrave in 1866, she was the daughter of William and Hannah Hargrave of Hollin House, High Hoyland. The couple went on to have three children, Thomas (1867-94), Charles (born 1869) and Herbert (1871-1940). Soon after Herbert's birth, his father, Thomas, became severely ill with lung problems and was advised by his own doctor to move to a drier climate as he would not survive in England's damp and rainy conditions. This was to tear the young family apart, Thomas elected to leave Britain and head for Utah in the United States, but his wife was unwilling to risk the lives of her children on such a journey and did not wish to be separated from her parents. With a heavy heart from both parties, Thomas boarded the *City of Brussels,* arriving in New York on 30 September 1872 alone, his youngest son was just 1 year old.

Utah had become the Mormon capital of the USA after Brigham Young had reached Salt Lake Valley in 1847. In the wider landscape, the Battle of Little Big Horn took place only four years after Thomas arrived in the country and famous, or perhaps more correctly infamous, characters such as Wyatt Earp (1848-1929), Billy the Kid (1859-81), Jesse James (1847-82), John Henry 'Doc' Holliday (1851-87), Sitting Bull (1831-90), Red Cloud (1822-1909), Annie Oakley (1860-1926) and 'Wild' Bill Hickok (1837-76) were very much alive and active. Indeed, the legendary gunfight at the OK Corral took place in 1881, and these events would have been breaking news to Thomas. Utah at this time had a total population of around 86,000 people, but more importantly featured a semi-arid-to-desert-type of climate, exactly what Thomas was looking for. He reputedly found work as a medic for the 'Cody Troop', formed by 'Buffalo Bill Cody' in 1883 as a way to preserve the history of the American way of life or 'the Wild West'. It consisted of a series of shows and performances of sharp shooting, horse riding and dramas depicting real life events. The first show opened in Omaha and went on to tour across the USA. Eventually, Cody brought the show to Europe, though it seems highly unlikely that Thomas was with them by then as he would almost certainly have made the effort to see his family.

Thomas did not give up trying to persuade Ann to join him and wrote numerous letters to her, though to no avail, and he spent the remainder of his long life in America before he died in about 1938 aged around 94. The whole saga left Ann very troubled as she made what she could of life living and bringing up her three boys at Hollin House aided by her mother and father. Thomas sent money from the States to support his family and all three boys received a good education. But the final twist to the story was Ann's untimely death in 1878 aged 37. Her children, aged 11, 9 and 7, were now solely brought up by Ann's parents. William Hargrave was born in 1810 and married his wife, Hannah, in 1838. He rented Hollin House Farm from the Stanhope family of Canon Hall, Cawthorne, and was noted to employ eleven labourers and two boys on his 97 acres in the 1871 census returns, he remained here until his death in 1897. William and Hannah's eldest daughter, Mary, married Charles Watson and they became the managers of the Scarsbrick Hotel in Southport, and so once a year the Hargrave family would leave Hollin House by horse and trap for a holiday by the sea, stopping *en route* to visit family in Glossop and Tintwhistle.

Thomas and Ann's three sons eventually left Hollin House. Thomas William Hargrave Turton ran a chemist shop in Stockton Heath, Warrington. Sadly, he was asthmatic and died on the premises in his twenties. Herbert made the long trip over to see his father and on his return brought a necklace and brooch for his future wife, Molly, hewn from rocks behind Niagara Falls, as a token of their engagement. Charles went one step further and travelled to Utah not only to see his father, but to stay there with him. In yet another tragedy to befall this family, Charles was killed in an accident involving one of the world's first combined harvesters.

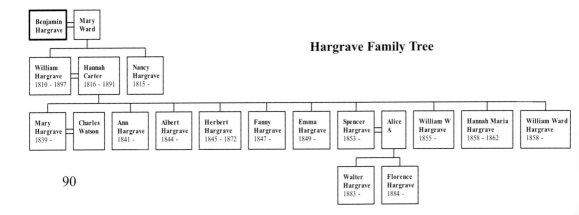

Hargrave Family Tree

Turton Family 1

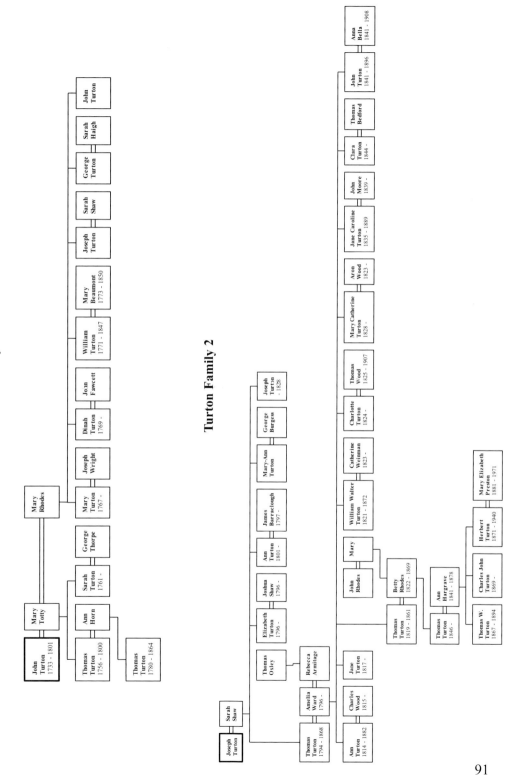

Turton Family 2

The earliest member of the family we currently know about is John Turton, who practised as a surgeon in Upper Denby. His son, also called Thomas, became a surgeon and apothecary, though he moved from Denby to live at Hatfield. His son, another Thomas, was born in 1780. He was admitted to Queen's College, Cambridge, in 1801 and moved to St Catherine's College in 1804. He graduated in 1805 and was elected a fellow of St Catherine's in 1806. He became Lucasian Professor of Mathematics from 1822 until 1826 and Regius Professor of Divinity from 1827 to 1842. By 1830 he was the Dean of Peterborough until 1842, then Dean of Westminster from 1842 to 1845. His final appointment was as the Bishop of Ely from 1845 to 1864, when he died. He was buried at Kensal Green Cemetery in the Royal Borough of Kensington and Chelsea. John Turton re-married after the death of his first wife and it is through his son, Joseph, who also became a surgeon, we can follow the family.

NB1: The above-mentioned William Turton and Mary Beaumont had the following family: Richard (1795-1871), Thomas (1796-1801), Harriot (1798-1876), Jane (1801-1874), Mynah (1804-1869), Dinah (1806-1884), Sarah (1806-1853), Mary (1808-1878), Thomas (1810-?), Zoah (1813-1874), Anne (1815-1847), Abigail (1816-1874), Elizabeth (1819-1886) and George (1821-1854).

NB2: George Turton, who married Sarah Haigh, lived at Bagden Lodge and was described in the census returns as a gentleman employing one servant.

Notes for Turton Family 2
1   Joseph Turton followed his father John's lead and became a surgeon.
2   Thomas Turton, who married Amelia Ward, lived at Pinfold, Denby, and also became a surgeon.
3   Elizabeth Turton (b.1796) married Joshua Shaw, who became the innkeeper of the Wagon & Horses by 1838, though by 1841 Elizabeth was running the pub on her own.
4   Ann Turton married Charles Wood, who was a member of the textile manufacturing dynasty that also brought Wesleyan Methodism to Denby Dale.
5   Jane Caroline Turton (b.1835) married John Moore, who was a member of the family of stonemasons from Upper Denby.
6   John Turton (b.1841) became a surgeon and chemist and lived at Plumpton House, Denby.
7   Thomas (b.1819) was apprenticed to his father and lived at Pinfold, Denby, until his death some time before 1861. He married Betty Rhodes, who came from Tintwistle. After Thomas died she returned to Tintwistle to live with her brother.

This Indenture, made the *Twenty sixth* day of *March* in the *fourth*

Year of the Reign of our Sovereign Lord WILLIAM the Fourth, by the Grace of God of the United Kingdom of Great Britain and Ireland, King, Defender of the Faith, and in the Year of our Lord One Thousand Eight Hundred and Thirty *four* BETWEEN *Thomas Turton the Elder of Denby in the Parish of Penistone in the County of York Surgeon and Apothecary* of the one part, and *Thomas Turton the Younger of Denby aforesaid, the Son of the said Thomas Turton the Older* of the other part; WITNESSETH, That the said *Thomas Turton the Younger*

An indenture produced for Doctor Thomas Turton (1794–1868) to train his son, Thomas Turton junior (1819–1861), as his apprentice, to follow his father into medicine, dated 1834.

Betty Turton, nee Rhodes, again. An older portrait of her but still dating to the 1860s.

Betty Turton, nee Rhodes, wife of Thomas Turton. Betty was born in 1822 and died in 1869, so this is an extremely early photograph.

Ann Hargrave, wife of Thomas Turton, who was born in 1841 and died in 1878, so this is another very old photograph.

93

A photograph of the Turton family, probably taken upon the occasion of Thomas Turton and Ann Hargrave's wedding in 1866. The children are currently unknown but the adults from left to right are: Thomas Turton (senior) 1794-1868, who can be seen with his newspaper, his second wife Rebecca Turton, nee Armitage, Ann Hargrave in the spotted dress (1841-1878), Hannah Hargrave, nee Carter (1816-1891), and William Hargrave (1810-1897), who was a farmer at Hollin House, High Hoyland.

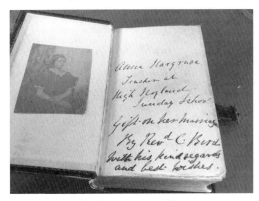

A prayer book given to Ann Hargarve on her wedding day to Thomas Turton in 1866. The inscription is by the rector of High Hoyland, Charles Bird.

Herbert Turton, son of Thomas and Ann Hargrave, with his wife, Mary Elizabeth Preston (known as Molly). Circa 1920.

A second photograph of the Turton family taken on the wedding day of Thomas Turton and Ann Hargrave. Top step: Hannah Hargrave, nee Carter, second step, Rebecca Turton, nee Armitage, and Thomas Turton (senior). Front step: The children are unknown but Thomas Turton Junior (1846-1942) is sitting and reading the newspaper.

The *City of Brussels*, the ship Thomas Turton boarded in 1872 for health reasons bound for New York. His wife, Ann, did not make the journey with him and they never saw each other again.

The necklace brought back by Herbert Turton from America as an engagement present for Mary Elizabeth (Molly) Preston. The gems were hewn from rocks behind Niagara Falls.

The British Legion – Denby Dale Branch

The British Legion was formed on 15 May 1921 and its purpose was to provide aid for ex-servicemen and their families who had had suffered as a result of serving in any branch of the armed forces during the war. Men who were wounded in battle might struggle to work in order to support their wives and children, and war widows faced a similar battle in the absence of their husbands. As a result of the war the UK's economy fell sharply and there were two million unemployed in 1921. Six million British men had fought in the war and 725,000 never returned. Of those who did, 1,750,000 had sustained disabilities and half were disabled. The Legion was the brainchild of Lance Bombardier Tom Lister who, in the absence of help from the government, took it upon himself to form an organisation to provide aid to those in unfortunate circumstances. The tradition of a two-minute silence to honour and remember the dead was already established by 1921, and the first poppy appeal took place in November of that year.

The records we have for the Denby Dale branch have only survived by chance. They were being stored in an old wooden box in the band room, which was about to be demolished during the 1970s. These consisted of minute books, dating from between 1921 to 1957, an account book, six contribution registers, a large number of completed application slips, and a few letters and notes, one of which makes mention of the sale of the Legion hut in 1940. I have only included annual activities such as poppy day, various local and national conferences and suchlike once in order to avoid repetition. There are also many instances of monetary relief and fund-raising activities, and the following is only a representative sample.

Membership slips

Those wishing to become a member of the British Legion had to complete application slips. The following table shows some of the details they supplied:

Wilfred Lockwood	Lower Denby	Royal Hampshire Reg.	4 June 1942	25 Jan. 1946	Private	Moulder
James Richard Kenyon	Broad Royd, Denby Dale	2. Duke of Wellington's Reg.	2 May 1945	17 Feb. 1948	Lieutenant	Student
Denis M Clegg	12 Leak Hall Cres., Denby Dale	HMS *Pembroke*	20 Sep. 1943	11 June 1947	Able Seaman	Joiner
Thomas William Alan Wilkinson	Fairleigh, Cumberworth	RAF	4 Aug. 1941	10 June 1946		Bank Clerk
Hubert Kilner	Rockwood Lodge, Denby Dale	Royal Engineers	2 July 1940	2 Feb. 1946	Sapper	Pipe Works Labourer
Denis J G Coppin	Lower Putting Hill, Denby Dale	54 Super Heavy Reg. R.Q. Field	15 Sep. 1939	2 May 1946	Gunner	Mechanic
John Ward	Olive Royd, Denby Dale	6th Bat. Highland Light Infantry	15 Jan. 1940	15 October 1945	Sergeant	Miner
Fred Peace	Dearneside, Denby Dale	Royal Army Service Corp	27 Nov. 1941	1 Oct. 1945	Private	Textiles
Granville Tucker	Water St. Scissett	Royal Army Service Corp	2 Jan. 1940	27 July 1946	Private	Butcher
Thomas Charlesworth	Upper Putting Hill, Denby Dale	Royal Artillery	22 Nov. 1939		Gunner	Miner
Selwyn Brian Simpson	1 Withy Side, Denby Dale	East Yorkshire Reg.	21 Jan. 1943	20 July 1946	Private	Charge Hand

A letter was sent from the British Legion, Northern Area at Durham to the Denby Dale branch on 9 March 1957. It was regarding Mr A Greensmith of 2 Wellthorne Avenue, Ingbirchworth. It was an enquiry about whether the wheelchair they issued for his use was still required.

The first minute book of the Denby Dale branch begins on 5 December 1921 when the committee met in the village band room. The first chairman was Rev Romeo Edwin Taglis of Upper Denby, the vice-chairman was Walter Heath (the village joiner). The secretary and treasurer was J A Loveday. Other committee members were: J Clarkson, C Kilner, J Morley, W Rowden and H Firth. The meeting was an inaugural one in which Edwin Hanson and Ernest Shaw were posted auditors and the bankers were to be Penistone branch of the Joint London City and Midland. An opening account balance of £20 6s 8d was deposited and the next meeting was to be held at the Denby Dale church hut a week later.

The minutes record sums of money granted to needy ex-servicemen.

Church Hut	9/1/1922	E Burdett of Stove End be granted £1 10s per week till the next meeting.
		Colin Herbert, Rest House, Denby be granted £1 per week for four weeks.
Church Hut	27/3/1922	Wallace Morley be granted 15s per week until next meeting.
Denby Dale	3/7/1922	The grant to Mrs Peace of Cumberworth be continued until next meeting.
Church School, Upper Denby	12/3/1923	That J Mosley be given authority to approach Dr Wilson with ref. To Mrs E E Pickering.
		That application for admission to convalescent home be made for the wife of Colin Herbert.
Band Room	5/4/1923	Resignation of W Rowden from this committee was considered and accepted.
Band Room	23/1/1924	That E Thorpe, Ingbirchworth be recommended for assistance, in kind, to be supplied by the Co-operative Stores, Denby Dale.
Band Room	26/5/1924	That Secretary, R Armitage write to late secretary Mr J A Loveday for all receipts, correspondence and anything belonging to the Fund, failure to comply with same request to be considered a slight on the committee.
Memorial Hall, Denby Dale	8/12/1925	No business.

NB: The committee also met at Denby Dale village school and the church school at Upper Denby.

By the date of the last meeting, Rev Taglis and the deputy, Walter Heath, who chaired far more meetings than the good Vicar of Denby, seem to have left the committee. The last meeting was presided over by J W Senior, and the rest of the minute book is blank.

By 1929, the Denby Dale branch of the Legion had moved on somewhat and the committee had accrued some of the village's wealthier inhabitants. In fact, the new president was a military veteran. Henry Gordon Cran (1889-1971) had moved into the village between the two world wars, occupying Rockwood House, which was originally built by Walter Norton (1833-1909). By 1909, it was reported that he be appointed a second-lieutenant in the Royal Field Artillery, though this appointment was to come later and he saw service throughout the First World War. In 1919, he married Dorothy Broadbent (1895-1949) in the Saddleworth district and they had two sons, William Broadbent Gordon Cran (1919-1972) and John Donald Cran. William also followed a military career and can be found with either the 122nd or

123rd Officer Cadet Training Unit in 1941. Later that year, he was commissioned as a captain with the Royal Regiment of Artillery, but was transferred in April 1942 to the Royal Army Ordnance Corps. In October 1942, he transferred again, this time to the Royal Electrical & Mechanical Engineers. In 1943/44, he served in Burma. He survived the war and returned home to marry Diana Rosemary Mallinson in 1945 at the Kings Chapel of Savoy in the Westminster district of London.

The Denby Dale Legion now had an experienced ex-officer as its figurehead alongside Norman and Algernon Hall (directors of Brownhill's textiles at Springfield Mill), Walter Kenyon (Dearneside Mills) and Major C H Stringer, another military man but one who seems to have been honorary as he never attended any meetings. The full list of officials in 1929 was as follows:

> *President – H G Cran*
> *Vice-presidents – N Hall, A F F Hall, A J Dare, W Kenyon, Major C H Stringer, Dr R N Farrar, Dr J T Bleasdell, Dr J Ness-Walker.*
>
> *Chairman – George Owen*
> *Vice-chairman – Joe Wray*
> *Joint general secretary & treasurer – J F Smith & F Shaw*
> *Relief secretary – Herbert Firth*
> *Pensions secretary – Joe Morley*
>
> *Local secretaries: Denby Dale – J W Senior; Scissett – J Barker; Clayton West – Jas. Smith.*
>
> *General Committee – Thos. Senior, George Hy. Lodge, Joe Birkinshaw, Charles Flack, Frank Leake, Charles Green, Sid. Dodd, James H Taylor, F Andrews, Ar. Hardcastle, Geo. Taylor, G W Hirst.*

Committee attendances in 1929 were recorded:

George Owen	24	Charles Flack	15
Frank Shaw	24	George Taylor	13
Joe Birkinshaw	23	Joe Wray	12
J F Smith	22	James H Taylor	12
J W Senior	22	H G Cran	11
Joe Barker	21	Charles Green	10
Jas. Smith	20	Thomas Senior	8
Herbert Firth	19	Frank Leake	7
Sid. Dodd	19	Joe Morley	4
A Hardcastle	17	F Andrews	3
Geo. Hy. Lodge	15	G W Hirst	0

NB: The Legion's meetings took place in the parish room at Scissett as well as the Victoria Memorial Hall, Denby Dale Band Hut and other venues.

British Legion,

Denby Dale & District Branch.

PRESIDENT - MR. H. G. CRAN.

Vice-Presidents:

Mr. N. Hall, Mr. A. F. F. Hall, Mr. A. J. Dare, Mr. W. Kenyon, Major C. H. Stringer, Dr. R. N. Farrar, Dr. J. T. Bleasdell, Dr. J. Ness-Walker.

Chairman—GEO. OWEN.

Vice-Chairman—JOE WRAY.

Joint General Secretary and Treasurer— J. F. SMITH & F. SHAW.

Relief Secretary—HERBERT FIRTH.

Pensions Secretary—JOE MORLEY

Local Secretaries—

Denby Dale—J. W. Senior.   Scissett—J. Barker.
Clayton West—Jas. Smith.

General Committee—

Thos. Senior, George Hy. Lodge, Joe Birkinshaw, Charles Flack, Frank Leake, Charles Green, Sid. Dodd, James H. Taylor, F. Andrews, Ar. Hardcastle, Geo. Taylor, G. W. Hirst.

E. M. Walker & Son, Printers, Crown Works, Clayton West.

Committee Attendances.

Meetings held, 24.

George Owen	...	24
Frank Shaw ...	...	24
Joe Birkinshaw	...	23
J. F. Smith ...	...	22
J. W. Senior...	...	22
Joe Barker ...	...	21
Jas. Smith ...	...	20
Herbert Firth	...	19
Sid. Dodd ...	...	19
A. Hardcastle	...	17
Geo. Hy. Lodge	...	15
Charles Flack	...	15
George Taylor	...	13
Joe Wray ...	...	12
James H. Taylor	...	12
H. G. Cran ...	...	11
Charles Green	...	10
Thomas Senior	...	8
Frank Leake...	...	7
Joe Morley ...	...	4
F. Andrews ...	...	3
G. W. Hirst ..	...	0

AGENDA.

Minutes of last General Meeting.

Business arising out of Minutes.

Balance Sheet.

Pensions Report.

U.S.F. and B.L.U.R.F. Report.

Election of Officers.

Any other Business.

It is hoped that all members of the Legion will do their best to attend the Annual General Meeting which will be held in the Parish Room, Scissett, on Tuesday, February 4th, 1930, at 7-30 p.m.

With the President's Compliments.

Denby Dale British Legion – Annual Report front cover and page 2.

BALANCE SHEET—January 1st to December 31st, 1929.

INCOME.	£	s.	d.	EXPENDITURE.	£	s.	d.
Cash brought forward	18	16	1½	Stationery		19	0
Cash in Bank	28	11	6	Printing		14	6
Bank Interest		17	6	Postages		15	10
Pension Secretary—in hand	1	1	11½	Affiliation Stamp Books	7	13	0
Members' Subscriptions ...	18	16	6	Printing Blocks		8	0
Badges Sold		10	0	Members' Cards		3	0
Tie Pin Badges sold... ...		11	0	Members' Hon. and Tie-Pin Badges		15	9
Diary Sold		1	0	Legion Journals		3	6
Whist Drive & Dance—Scissett	3	5	10	Branch Standard, Sling and Cover	11	1	0
Armistice Service—Denby Dale	4	0	3	Dedication Sheets		4	3
„ „ Clayton West ..		18	0	3 Wreaths Haig's Memorial ...	1	10	0
Whist Drive—Denby Dale ...	4	0	2	1 Member's Wreath		10	0
Contributions to Standard		1	0	1 Wreath in hand		10	0
Grant from Denby Dale Pie Com....	5	10	0	Cupboard ... .: ...	1	12	6
				Rent of Branch Rooms ...		10	0
				Dinner Expenses—Feb. 1929 ...	1	1	6
				Relief Secretary's Expenses ...		4	11½
				Parade Advt.—D.V.A. ...		4	0
				Dinner Expenses, Dec. 1929 ...	1	1	6
				Grant from D. Dale Pie Committee			
				Transferred to Special Relief Fund	5	10	0
				Cash in hand	1	16	1
				Cash in Bank	32	8	0
				Pension Sec.—Cash in hand ...	1	1	11½
				Cash in hands of Sub. Secs. and due			
				from Whist Drive, D. Dale ...	16	0	0
	£87	0	10		£87	0	10

Audited and found Correct, January 21st, 1930.

JAMES HAYDN TAYLOR
JOE WRAY.

Denby Dale British Legion – Annual Report – Balance Sheet.

By 1929, meetings always began with a minute's silence. The minutes always record who was in the chair, usually George Owen but occasionally Henry Gordon Cran. The minutes of the last meeting were read and approved then any correspondence was read out and discussed, followed by varying reports from different departments, requests for aid and fund-raising events. The minutes still record individual cases concerning the requirements of local veterans and their families. Of course, in order to be able to give financial relief and pay out pensions, the Legion had to raise funds, and some of the more interesting minutes follow.

> ### Notes from a meeting held Tuesday 18 November 1929:
> ### Case – E Burdett.
> *The Secretary had seen this man and that all the children being in hospital there could be no assistance granted. Since the Relief Secretary saw this man he has lost his wife so the committee asked the Relief Secretary what assistance could be granted which he promised to carry out.*
>
> ### Poppy Day Collections.
> *The President now informed the committee that the poppy sale was a success and that the street collection was £51 9s 4½d with the poppy's [sic] sold for the wreath made the total to £54 4s 10d.*
>
> ### Notes from a meeting held Tuesday 3 December 1929:
> *In view of the fact that the President had intimated that for the forthcoming year he would be unable to give much of his time to the Legion and had suggested that we should elect a new President, Mr S Dodd moved and Mr J Barker seconded, that this committee places all confidence in Mr Cran and that we cannot entertain his suggestion.*
>
> ### Notes from a meeting held Tuesday 15 April 1930:
> *The President reported that the date mentioned for holding the proposed rally at Bretton, Lord Allendale would be away in camp with his regiment. The President reported that he had been to see the Earl of Harewood's secretary with a view to holding it there if it were fixed up to holding it on that date and it was his intention to try and get the Prince of Wales while he was up North (to attend).*
>
> ### Notes from a meeting held Tuesday 15 July 1930:
> *At this point the President stated that owing to some circumstances (personal) the proposed Garden Party which was to be held at Rockwood on Saturday August 9th 1930, would have to be postponed,*

but asked that the subject be left open for discussion on some future date.

An invitation to the Legion was given by the St. Johns Ambulance Brigade to attend their annual service on Sunday July 27th 1930 at Denby Dale which was accepted.

Mr Cran proposed and Mr Joe Wray seconded that we write to the Society Steward of the Wesleyan Church, Denby Dale (Mr J W Rowley) re. The coming of their new Minister and ask him to inform the Minister of our Annual Armistice Service on the Sunday preceding November 11th. It was also decided to invite the Minister to give the address on that day.

Notes from a meeting held Tuesday 12 May 1931:
The area Rally at Harewood came up for discussion next and the secretary was asked to write to various bus companies with regard to quoting prices for a trip there from the branch.

Notes from a meeting held Tuesday 19 May 1931:
The Rally was the next business for discussion. That we book Messrs. Hirst Bros., Denby Dale for the trip at 4s per head for 30 or more. (The charge for this was £14.)

Notes from a meeting held Tuesday 18 August 1931:
On behalf of the Ambulance Brigade Mr Joe Wray thanked the Legion members who turned out at their annual parade and service at Denby Dale. Whilst this was appreciated it was deplored that the number was only too few considering the Ambulance turn out at our Annual Memorial Services.

Notes from a meeting held Tuesday 1 September 1931:
Whist Drive at Scissett, October 6 in the Parish Room That we get 25 posters and 100 tickets from Mary Bell. The Secretary was instructed to write to the following with a view to getting the whist prizes, Major Stringer, R J H Beanland, G H Norton, Noel Beardsell, J Dews, H Auckland and Dr Farrar. (Various replies were received by the following meeting – G H Norton promised a rug, R J H Beanland sent 10s, Dr Farrar 5s and Major Stringer 10s.)

Notes from a meeting held Tuesday 10 November 1931:
Annual Dinner. It was decided to have 100 tickets for the dinner and J W Rowley was instructed to have same printed. The Secretary was

instructed to invite the following guests to the dinner: Rev. A Walkden, A Bleasby, F Bryan Holmes, Honorary Life Members: Rev. H C Libby, J Brownhill, G H Norton, G W Naylor, Vice-Presidents: Rev. N G Hounsfield, Dr Farrar, Dr Bleasdell, Major C H Stringer, W Kenyon, A Hall. (The venue was the Crown Hotel in Scissett.)

Notes from a meeting held Tuesday 8 December 1931:
The following were submitted and passed for Christmas Parcels from Special Relief Funds, the amount to be 10s each parcel:–

Fred Priest (Denby Dale), Thomas Senior, W H Boyce (Lower Cumberworth), James Smith (Clayton West), William Carter, G Buckley (Lower Denby).

Notes from a meeting held 5 April 1932:
After discussion it was decided to be represented at the Annual Conference at Portsmouth, on the motion of A Taylor, seconded by C Ibbotson, the sum of 12s 6d per day to be allowed plus rail fare. (The General Secretary was chosen to go who at this point was H Firth.)

Notes from a meeting held Tuesday 15 November 1932:
Typhoid epidemic at Denby Dale. This matter was discussed and it was moved by J Smith and seconded by J W Senior that we forward a donation of £5 from the Branch Fund to the Distress Fund which has been opened at Denby Dale. Notification to be forwarded to Headquarters.

Notes from a meeting held 25 April 1933:
The secretary was instructed to write to Messrs. Stringer & Son on behalf of A Booth asking that should a vacancy arise would they consider this man, who was a disabled ex-serviceman and one of their former employees, who was discharged when the Skelmanthorpe coke ovens was closed down.

Notes from a meeting held 12 September 1933:
Denby & Cumberworth Water Scheme. It was proposed by J W Rowley and seconded by J Smith that the Secretary write to the Clerk to the Denby and Cumberworth UDC re. Additions to water supply and ask if this is a state aided scheme and if so the proportion of ex-servicemen it is proposed to employ as it is the desire of the Legion that the full quota be employed if suitable. (The reply arrived before the next week's meeting and was not considered satisfactory so the matter was handed

over to one of the district councillors to bring before the council at their next meeting.)

It was proposed by J F Smith and seconded by F Smith that we send a wreath to the interment of Sir James Hinchliffe who had been a member of pensions and other committees in connection with ex-servicemen.

Notes from a meeting held 16 January 1934:
Re. Talking Pictures. It was decided to apply for the talking picture film to be shown at the Scissett Parish Room. Dates to be suggested Feb 5 or 7. (It took until 4 April before the unknown film was actually shown.)

Notes from a meeting held 20 February 1934:
After the meeting the President gave a very interesting account of his recent visit to France and Belgium. He said that many English ex-servicemen were settled in the various districts. He gave a brief account of the state of the various battlefields and cemeteries and commented on the excellent state of repair and tidiness of the cemeteries. The account was enjoyed by all.

Notes from a meeting held 29 May 1934:
Re. Proposed widening of the road at Scissett. M Firth proposed and H Schofield seconded that the Secretary write to the Manager Employment Exchange Skelmanthorpe for names of ex-servicemen who are registered as unemployed in order to be able to place before the authorities such names asking that they may be employed in the proposed road widening at Scissett.

Notes from a meeting held 2 October 1934:
Unemployment Officers circular was read and it was decided to recommend Frank Hirst, Denby Dale, if still unemployed for Christmas postal work.

Notes from a meeting held 16 April 1935:
It was proposed by R Poole and seconded by J Barker that we forward a donation of £2 to the Denby Dale Council towards the proposed improvements to the War Memorial grounds.

Notes from a meeting held 14 May 1935:
The President Mr Cran, informed the meeting that he had received from Mr Waldo Briggs on behalf of the Branch two etchings, one of Earl

Haigh and one of Lord Kitchener. It was decided to hang them in the Committee room and the Secretary was instructed to forward the grateful thanks of the Branch for this splendid gift.

It was also decided on the motion of J F Smith, seconded by A Taylor, that we also have a photograph of our late President Dr Archibald and the present President Mr Cran and that these photographs be placed in the Committee room in addition.

Notes from a meeting held 18 June 1935:
It was proposed by J F Smith and seconded by J W Senior that we have a photograph of the Committee and Branch, this to be taken on some future date at a garden party if possible.

Notes from a meeting held 3 September 1935:
Photograph. The replies re. Photograph being considered satisfactory it was proposed by Mr Cran and seconded by J F Smith that we proceed with the matter and the Secretary make arrangements with Mr F Biltcliffe of Skelmanthorpe re. Same.

Notes from a meeting held 17 September 1935:
Photograph. Proofs of the photograph of members were examined and it was decided to order 6 dozen postcards, the question of an enlargement for the Branch to be left over at present. (By the next meeting the 6 dozen postcards had all sold and a further 2 dozen were ordered.)

Notes from Annual General Meeting Monday 26 October 1936:
Election of Officers.
President – Mr Cran was re-elected unanimously.

Vice-Presidents – Messrs. A F F Hall, W Kenyon, Capt. Brewer, C E Moxon, Major Eager, Colonel Burbury, Dr R M Farrar, Rev. N G Hounsfield were re-elected en bloc *on the motion of G Owen seconded by J W Senior.*

Chairman – Mr G Owen was proposed for Chairman by Mr Cran, seconded by J W Senior. An amendment that J W Rowley be Chairman was moved by G Owen, seconded by N Ibbotson. A vote was taken and G Owen was declared elected Chairman for the next year.

Vice-Chairman – Mr J W Rowley was proposed for Vice-Chairman by J Wray, seconded by F Senior. An amendment was made that J Wray be Vice-Chairman, proposed by A Taylor, seconded J W Senior. On a vote being taken J W Rowley was declared elected.

Honorary Secretary – H Firth was proposed for Hon. Sec. By J W Rowley seconded by F Senior, an amendment that N Ibbotson be Hon. Sec. Was made by F Shaw seconded by R Poole. On a vote being taken H Firth was declared elected.

Hon. Treasurer – J W Senior was elected Hon. Treasurer on the motion of A Taylor, seconded by F Shaw.

Hon. Relief Secretary – N Ibbotson was elected Hon. Relief Secretary on the motion of H Firth, seconded by F Senior.

Hon. Pensions Secretary – J Wray was elected Hon. Pensions Secretary on the motion of Mr Cran, seconded by J W Rowley.

General Committee – J F Smith, F Shaw, J H Taylor, G Taylor, C Ibbotson, S Wood, A Taylor, F Senior, R Poole, J Irvine, B Swannick, F Bintcliffe were elected as General Committee on the motion of J W Rowley, seconded by G Owen.

Members of the Denby Dale branch of the British Legion in 1930

Henry Gordon Cran	Joseph White	B Broadbent
Dr Bleasdell	William Woofenden	Dr J Ness Walker
W H Kenyon	C A Hanwell	W Turton
George Owen	Fred Bower	George Lukes
Thomas Senior	H Wilkinson	Norman Lodge
J W Cunningham	James Lodge	Arnold Ellis
G J M Lee	Rowland Potter	F Andrews
Fred Hirst	John Phillips	Frank Hirst
Joe Mosley	John Robinson	Harry Bell
S F Goodwin	Harry Lawton	Wilfred Mosley
Thomas Lockwood	Sykes Wood	George Priest
J W Senior	A J Rhodes	Darcy Birkett
Ernest Burdett	A Holt	Harry Schofield
Arthur Priest	Thomas Edward Fisher	Thomas Peace
G W Hirst	Theodore Walters	Moorhouse Kaye
Charlie Flack	Fred Jubb	Vincent Peace
G W Hallas	H Burman	Clarence Ibbotson
Luther Lockwood	Arthur Smith	Joe Dyson
George Senior	Colin Herbert *[crossed out]*	Harold Stephenson
Norman Whiteley	Fred Priest	John Rowley
Thomas Fretwell	Hayden Littlewood	
Clarence Ibbotson *[crossed out]*	Algernon F F Hall	

Notes from a meeting held 15 December 1936:
Trip to London at Whitsuntide 1937. A letter was received from Dean & Dawson asking that owing to the situation which had arisen through King Edwards [sic] abdication did the branch intend to carry on with the trip as before. It was moved that we are carrying on and the Secretary notify Dean & Dawson to this effect.

Notes from a meeting held 4 May 1936:
It was reported to the meeting that A Tolhurst had received an offer of employment for the hop picking season in Kent. As this man has been off work for a long period it was moved that we grant 10s from the Special Relief Fund towards fare.

Notes from a meeting held 25 May 1937:
The collecting boxes in connection with the Coronation Appeal were opened and contents counted and the amount realised was £7 7s 4d including the collection from Coronation Service at Denby Dale. This was considered satisfactory.

Notes from a meeting held 15 February 1938:
It was moved by F Shaw, seconded by J W Senior that Mr Harold Hinchliffe, Denby Dale be elected Vice-President of the Branch.

Notes from a meeting held 26 April 1938:
The Secretary reported that at the suggestion of the President a letter of sympathy had been sent to Mr Brownhill in regard to the death of his son Capt. C Brownhill in South Africa. A letter in reply received from Mr Brownhill was read thanking the members for their sympathy.

Notes from a meeting held 17 May 1938:
A letter was read from the President, Mr Cran, stating he was entering a nursing home for treatment. The Secretary was instructed to reply expressing the members' sympathy and wishing him a speedy and complete recovery.

By 1937/38 there had been a few changes in personnel on the committee, though plenty of the older faces were still there as recorded in the AGM pamphlet.

President – H Gordon Cran
Vice Presidents – A F F Hall, W Kenyon, C E Moxon, Harold Hinchliffe,

Rev. N G Hounsfield, F Andrew, Herbert Hinchliffe.
Chairman – George Owen
Vice Chairman – J W Rowley
Honorary General Secretary – Herbert Firth
Honorary Treasurer – J W Senior
Honorary Relief Secretary – A Taylor
Honorary Pensions Secretary – J Wray
General Committee – James Smith, J F Smith, F Shaw, N Ibbotson, C Ibbotson, J Irvine, G Taylor, S Wood, F Senior, R Poole, G Hallas, J H Taylor, J H Swannick, H Peace, C Flack, S Ellis.

The pamphlet continues:

Will all members do their best to attend in the Branch Room over the Conservative Club, Scissett on Tuesday 29 November 1938 at 7:30pm.
During the last year assistance to the value of £12 10s 2d has been issued to cases caused through sickness and unemployment. Convalescent treatment at Lowestoft and Southport and fares to same. Also two Educational Outfits.

The Second World War years
The United Kingdom declared war on Germany on 3 September 1939, only 21 years after the conclusion of the First World War and only eighteen since the British Legion had been founded.

Notes from a meeting held 26 September 1939:
A resolution was moved by J W Rowley and seconded by J Smith that the Secretary obtain from the Labour Exchange the names of the ex-servicemen who are unemployed as it is felt that some of the ARP duties could be done by ex-servicemen thus releasing younger men for other duties.
It was moved by J Smith and seconded by J F Smith that we carry on with Poppy Day arrangements.

Notes from a meeting held 10 October 1939:
Remembrance Services. It was suggested that owing to the present conditions, it was not considered advisable to hold the parade this year, but that short services and laying of wreaths be held at each district War Memorial.

Notes from AGM held 21 October 1939:
The President (Henry Gordon Cran), then addressed the meeting and stated that twelve months ago we little thought we should again be meeting under war conditions. It was satisfactory to note that the Branch had carried on during the past year and dealt with matters which had arisen. The duties of the Legion would be much more heavy during the coming periods owing to the number of young men being called to the services. The matter of parents [sic] allowances and pensions in case of disability would have to be dealt with and advice and assistance would be required, which he hoped the Legion would be able to give.

Notes from a meeting held 14 November 1939:
Meeting to count unsold poppies and monies collected. Amount, including Church collections £83 12d 3d, as follows:

Street collections by Branch – £74 4d 7d
Denby Dale Holy Trinity Church – £2 6s
Denby St. Johns – £1 15s 7d
Cumberworth St. Nicholas – £3 6d
Clayton West All Saints – £1 10s 9d
Bretton Park Chapel – 9s 4d

Notes from a meeting held 12 February 1940:
Owing to difficulties of rationing and black out travelling it was agreed unanimously to leave the question of the annual dinner over for the present.

At a meeting held on 12 March 1940, a subtle but important change was made by the Legion regarding recording the minute's silence in the minute book. The words were now expressed thus: 'The meeting opened with the silent tribute to fallen comrades.' No doubt this change was brought about because of the ongoing hostilities in Europe. The Legion had also reduced their weekly meetings to monthly ones.

Notes from a meeting held 4 June 1940:
Owing to members of the committee having to report for LDV duties the meeting was concluded and the next meeting was arranged for 25 June.

Notes from a meeting held 6 August 1940:
The Secretary was instructed to write to Rev. Hounsfield expressing the

pleasure of the committee and members, on hearing the good news that his son was alive, although a prisoner, instead of being killed as at first reported.

Notes from a meeting held 22 October 1940:
A letter was read out from Rev. Briggs, Denby Dale, re Armistice and it was agreed that Rev. Briggs arrange the service and invite all other denominations and Home Guards and Voluntary Services.

Notes from a meeting held 14 January 1941:
A circular letter which had been drawn up by the Secretary was read and approved. This was to be given to all serving soldiers from our district with a view of admitting them to the Legion as Honorary members while serving and then full membership on discharge or demobilisation. It was proposed by J W Rowley and seconded by A Douglas that we have 500 copies printed.

Receipt slip for a donation of £101 made by the Denby Dale British Legion in 1942 to the Earl Haigh Appeal Fund.

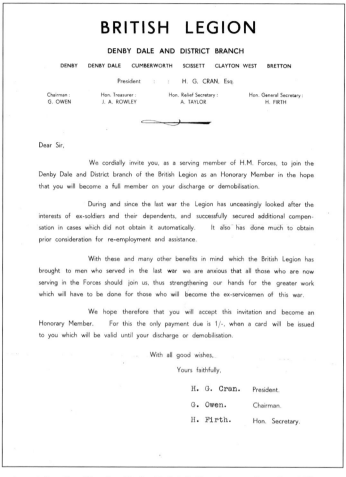

BRITISH LEGION

DENBY DALE AND DISTRICT BRANCH

DENBY   DENBY DALE   CUMBERWORTH   SCISSETT   CLAYTON WEST   BRETTON

President   :   :   H. G. CRAN, Esq.

Chairman :	Hon. Treasurer :	Hon. Relief Secretary :	Hon. General Secretary :
G. OWEN	J. A. ROWLEY	A. TAYLOR	H. FIRTH

Dear Sir,

We cordially invite you, as a serving member of H.M. Forces, to join the Denby Dale and District branch of the British Legion as an Honorary Member in the hope that you will become a full member on your discharge or demobilisation.

During and since the last war the Legion has unceasingly looked after the interests of ex-soldiers and their dependents, and successfully secured additional compensation in cases which did not obtain it automatically. It also has done much to obtain prior consideration for re-employment and assistance.

With these and many other benefits in mind which the British Legion has brought to men who served in the last war we are anxious that all those who are now serving in the Forces should join us, thus strengthening our hands for the greater work which will have to be done for those who will become the ex-servicemen of this war.

We hope therefore that you will accept this invitation and become an Honorary Member. For this the only payment due is 1/-, when a card will be issued to you which will be valid until your discharge or demobilisation.

With all good wishes,

Yours faithfully,

H. G. Cran.   President.

G. Owen.   Chairman.

H. Firth.   Hon. Secretary.

A circular sent out by the Denby Dale British Legion to local soldiers serving in the Second World War inviting them to become honorary members in the hope that at the end of hostilities they would become full members.

Notes from AGM held 2 December 1941:
A letter was read from the President, Mr Cran, expressing his apologies for not being able to be present owing to illness as he was now in a nursing home. He also apologised for not having been able to attend meetings regularly owing to difficulties of travelling, petrol restrictions and illness. He expressed a wish that someone else should be elected President owing to the above mentioned difficulties.

Notes from AGM held 15 December 1942:
The membership now stands at 107. Honorary Members serving in the forces number 222, of which 80 had joined in the past year.

Notes from a meeting held 12 January 1943:
Women's Land Army. It was reported that Miss Mary Swannick, a member of the Women's Timber Corps who had been injured whilst working had been charged for hospital treatment and on discharge from hospital had been sent home. No arrangements had been made for pay and she had not had any payment for some weeks. The Secretary was instructed to write to the WLA Welfare Officer regarding the case.

Notes from a meeting held 13 April 1943:
Notification was read re C Tinker who had died whilst a prisoner of war in Tripoli. This stated that the Ministry of Pensions had admitted that death was attributable to war service and that the parents would be entitled to pension if circumstances warrant same. This information has been given to the family for consideration.

The Secretary reported that he had been visited by F Atkinson who has been discharged from the Navy after receiving injuries. He states that in his opinion his assessment for pension is low and would like an appeal to be made by the Branch for re-assessment if possible. The Secretary stated he had forwarded a letter of enquiry to Headquarters Pension Dept. for their opinion and advice.

Notes from a meeting held 11 May 1943:
A reply was read re application on behalf of Mr F Atkinson. This stated that the Pensions Dept. were submitting a claim for increased pension and they would inform us as soon as possible of the result. The Chairman informed the meeting that he had invited Mr F Atkinson, a discharged naval man to attend, with a view to joining the committee as it is desired that the men of the present war take part in the Legions [sic] activities as it is expected that a large number of cases of disability, sickness etc. will arise from the present war. Mr Atkinson, who was present, expressed his willingness to join the committee.

Notes from a meeting held 8 June 1943:
A letter was read from Capt. Wilcox, Poppy Day organiser, asking that supplies be ordered early in order to avoid damage by possible air raids. The Secretary was instructed to order the same amount as last year as soon as possible.

PHONE : RICHMOND 0183.   TELEGRAMS : BRITEGION, RICHMOND.

BRITISH LEGION
(Incorporated by Royal Charter.)
FOUNDED BY THE LATE FIELD MARSHAL EARL HAIG (1921).
PATRON :
HIS MAJESTY THE KING.

PRESIDENT :   VICE-CHAIRMAN :
MAJ.-GEN. SIR F. MAURICE, K.C.M.G., C.B.   LT.-COL. SIR IAN FRASER, C.B.E., M.P.
CHAIRMAN :   HON. TREASURER :
BRIG.-GEN. E. R. FITZPATRICK, C.B.E., D.S.O., D.L.   MAJOR SIR BRUNEL COHEN.
NATIONAL EMERGENCY ADDRESS   CARDIGAN HOUSE RICHMOND HILL, Sy.
GENERAL SECRETARY : MR. J. R. GRIFFIN.
Your Ref._____   Our Ref._E._

                                        7th October, 1944.

The Hon. Secretary,
British Legion,
Denby Dale &District Branch,
Kitchenroyd,
Denby Dale,
Huddersfield.

Dear Sir,

    In reply to your letter of the 2nd, compassionate
leave is seldom granted to a man serving overseas on
compassionate grounds unless there are very except-
ional circumstances.

    The relatives of the serving soldier concerned,
should write to the Under Secretary of State, War
Office, London, S.W.1. (A.G.4.A.) requesting that
consideration may be given in respect of compassionate
leave. The application should be supported with
medical evidence in regard to the father.

                        Yours faithfully,

                        AGWebb

              EMPLOYMENT AND PENSIONS DEPARTMENT.
T/JS.

A letter from the British Legion headquarters regarding a communication by the Denby Dale British Legion about compassionate leave dated 1944.

1944 POPPY DAY REPORT.
The undermentioned are particulars extracted from our files, and will be
included in our records failing the receipt of additions or amendments.
Please see accompanying letter.

District   DENBY DALE.

County   W.R.YORKS.   A.D. Ref. No. 63.

Denby Dale.   92. 10. 6.

    Sale of Poppies, etc.   83. 7. 0.
    Centenary Methd Church.   4. 7. 0.
    All Saints Church.   3. 0. 6.
        "   "   " Bretton.   16. 0.
    Donations.   1. 0. 0.

In giving details of Church Collections
please state denomination in each case.

Communications on this subject should be addressed to
Captain W. G. WILLCOX, M.B.E., Organising Secretary,
Earl Haig's British Legion Appeal, Cardigan House, Richmond Hill,
Richmond, Surrey.

DUPLICATE
TO BE KEPT FOR REFERENCE
BY HONORARY ORGANISER

1945

Ref. No.	Item.	Min. Selling Price	Quantity.
1	Small Poppies	3d.	2000
2	Silk Poppies (Small)	6d.	2000
3	Silk Poppies (Large)	1/-	780
4	Giant Poppies	2/6	20
5	Mascots		5
6	Remembrance Crosses	6d.	12
7	Small Posters, size 30 x 20 ins.		
8	Window Bills, circular, 9½ins. diameter		
9	Motor Car Bills, size 5 x 9 ins.		12
10	Leaflets		
11	Lantern Slides for Cinemas, sets of		
12	Collecting Boxes (unlabelled)		
13	Collecting Box Labels		50
14	Trays ... Small.		12
15	Collectors' Badges		50
16	House-to-House Collectors' Certificates		50
17			
18			
19			
20			
21			
22			

URGENT.

The ORDER FORM on left should be completed and returned
as soon as possible to :—

            Captain W. G. Willcox, M.B.E.,

                Organising Secretary,

                    HAIG'S FUND,

                        Richmond, Surrey.

Telephone : Richmond 0131.

Telegrams : DETHONOUR, RICHMOND, SURREY.

KEEP THIS COPY FOR REFERENCE

A receipt dated 1945 for supplies bought by the Denby Dale British Legion for their annual poppy day.

A summary of poppy day sales and donations dating to the early 1940s.

Notes from a meeting held 11 July 1944:
Two local serving men, having been mentioned in dispatches it was moved that a letter of congratulation be sent to each with the good wishes of the members of the Branch. The two men are R N Rowley (son of the Treasurer) and Harold Shaw.

NB: These men may have been mentioned for their actions in Northern France as D-Day took place on 6 June 1944.

As the war drew to a close the number of men being accepted as new members of the Legion increased regularly as they were demobbed from the services. This peaked around Spring 1946. The members for the year 1945-1946 were as follows:

Cran H G	Ibbotson C	Walker F
Kenyon W	Ibbotson N	
Hall A F F	Peace V G	Newly Recruited:
Andrew F	Kaye M	Rhodes E C
Moxon C H	Kendal F	Poulter G
Hinchliffe Hld.	Leake C	Sleaford L
Hinchcliffe Hbt.	Leake F	Wray H
Ackroyd Hbt.	Law H	Elms F G
Addy P	Lockwood C	Wilkie D A
Astwick F	Lockwood A	Wade C C
Adsetts A	Lodge G H	Blacker G D
Atkinson F	Lee G T	Priest G
Astwick H	Loveday J	Poole R
Booth Ern.	Lawton H	Peace J F
Brooke Roy	Lawton K	Pell W
Broadbent B	Littlewood I	Pillinger J
Barber A	Mitchell A	Swannick E C
Blacker B	Mosley C	Swannick H A
Bower F	Mommen E L	Eastwood W
Battye F	Matthews J	Turton G H
Battye A	Nelson H	Tucker A
Burton H	Noble S	Tucker C E
Bentley A	Newsome P R	Tucker D
Barker R	Owen G	Borthwick J E
Berry G	Ormondroyd L	Beaumont R
Bowden H	Poulter R	Hallas J R
Barraclough J	Poulter H	Coulton A

Bridge I
Blackburn D
Bostwick G A
Carter W
Chilton F
Clarke W
Cooke F
Coldwell B
Craven A
Clough G
Copley S
Dobson R
Douglas H
Douglas A
Downend G
Dearnley L
Douglas A D
Ellis S
England W
Flack D
Fish G W
Firth H (Jun.)
Firth H (Sen.)
Firth A
Fretwell D
Garthwaite D
Glover Thos.
Greaves F
Gunson C
Gunson A
Hey P
Holmes W
Hirst F
Hirst Hbt.
Hirst G W
Hirst C H
Hirst N
Hirst J W
Haigh C
Hallas W G

Robinson E
Rowley J W
Rowley J A
Rowley C
Robinson C H
Robinson W H
Rowley E
Robinson D
Robinson L
Rowley Clifford
Rowley R V
Senior J W
Senior Thos.
Senior G
Senior F
Smith J F
Smith J
Stott G
Sheard A E
Shaw F
Shaw N
Swannick J H
Schofield H
Stanley J P
Skurls W
Smith G W
Smith Hy.
Smith C E
Shaw A
Tingay C
Taylor J H
Taylor G
Taylor W R
Tinsley A
Turton W
Turton H
Taylor C
Taylor C S
Woffinden W
Wood Sykes

Shaw Ed.
Bellwood D
Roberts H
Craven L
Ormondroyd W
Auty R W
Haigh L S
Mallinson G
Rhodes G W
Shaw Eric
Pell Gilbert
Lodge Colin
Mitchell Harvey
Hill Jack
Craven Kenneth
Rusby Thomas
Littlewood Arthur
Scott Alec
Newton Eric
Bank Clifford
Lockwood Walter
Whittle W J S
Clarkson C
Cudworth Brian
Haigh J M
Fisher F R
Taylor W H
Brown Walter
White Alec
Garthwaite S
Summers E
Ackroyd J M
Hanwell Ernest
Buckly W R
Nelson Harold
Dransfield Arnold
Swift Ronald
Blackburn Harry
Bailey W
Hirst Robert

Hall H	Wood Sam	Dickinson Rufus
Heeley C	Wray J	Burton J
Hargrave B	Whitlam S	
Haigh N	Woodhead F	
Hall W	Whittaker S	
Hardy F W	Wood Ronnie	

NB: The above list is exactly as taken from the contribution ledger but as soldiers were being demobbed in 1946 they had, in the main, their Christian names recorded rather than just their initial.

Notes from a meeting held 22 January 1946:
A proposition by Mr C E Moxon and seconded by J F Smith. That it would be in the best interests of the British Legion and ex-servicemen in the District to have two branches in place of the present Denby Dale & District Branch owing to distance and difficulty of contact between members. This was discussed and it was agreed to consider the resolution at the Committee Meeting to be held 26 February.

Notes from a meeting dated 12 March 1946:
Two members, Mr J Smith and J W Bell having attained the age of seventy years, it was moved and seconded that they become life members of the Legion and that no further contributions be paid by them.

Notes from a meeting held 23 July 1946:
The President, Mr Cran, informed the meeting that he would like the committee to be his guests at a private dinner, as after the year end two Branches would be in the place of the present one.

Notes from a meeting held in the Memorial Hall, 5 November 1946:
In his remarks the President, Mr Cran, informed the meeting that the Clayton West members had decided to start a new Branch, therefore the present Branch as constituted previously would have to be re-organised. He asked for a proposition that this should be carried out and it was proposed by G Owen and seconded by G J M Lee that the new area should consist of Denby Dale, Upper & Lower Cumberworth, Denby and Birdsedge.

The following officials were elected for the coming year:
Chairman – H G Cran, Vice Chairman – G Wright, Hon. Treasurer – N Turton, Hon. Secretary – H Firth, Hon. Assistant Secretary – M Kaye.

It was unanimously agreed to invite Dr D E Mitchell to become President and the Secretary was instructed to write to him informing him of this decision and state that a deputation would see him if necessary.

Notes from a meeting held 18 November 1946:

With reference to the invitation to Dr Mitchell to become President, the Secretary read a letter from Dr Mitchell accepting and thanking the members for the invitation.

The Secretary reported that he had received a letter from the Denby Dale Urban District Council asking for the names of the fallen in the 1939-45 War in the area covered by the Branch as it was proposed that the Council undertake the work [on the memorial], *if sanctioned by the Ministry of Health. The Secretary then reported that this had been done and names forwarded as requested. A further letter was then read out stating that the Ministry of Health would not sanction the expenditure and suggesting that the cost be met by a public appeal as with the case of Emley where the names had already been inscribed on the local Memorial.*

Arising from the above letter it was moved and agreed that the Secretary write to Messrs. E T Moore & Son, Thurlstone Road, Penistone, the erectors of the Denby Dale Cenotaph for an estimate of the cost of the inscription in the same style and lettering as those already on and also the probable time for completion if engaged.

The committee elected for the year ahead:
Chairman – H G Cran, Vice Chairman – G E Wright. Members: G Owen, W J Whittle, G E Fish, A Smith, L Tarbatt, T Thackra, W Bedford, Sykes Wood, J W Rowley, R Hirst, W Bailey.

Notes from a meeting held at the Memorial Hall 3 December 1946:

A letter was read from the Secretary of the Memorial Hall Trustees stating that the cost of the room for meetings would be 4s per meeting. No objection would be raised to putting a cupboard in the room for storage purposes.

It was moved by W J Whittle that an account for Branch funds be opened with the Yorkshire Penny Bank, Denby Dale Branch.

Notes from a meeting held 26 August 1947:
The Secretary reported that application had been made to Ministry of Pensions for forms of application for pension on behalf of John Gaunt, Upper Denby. The grant issued to J Gaunt, Denby, having expired and the period allowed by local committees having being granted it was agreed that this case should be referred to Headquarters for their consideration and action.

Notes from a meeting held 9 September 1947:
In reply to the application re J Gaunt a reply was received from Area authorising a further grant. It was moved that eight weeks grant at £1 weekly be allowed.

Notes from a meeting held 23 September 1947:
A letter was read from the Secretary of the Denby Dale Brass Band re our application for the legion cupboard to be placed in the band room at a rental of 10s per year and meetings at 2s 6d each.

Notes from a meeting held 2 December 1947:
It was moved by N Turton and seconded by M Kaye that W J P Whittle be chairman. (Former president and chairman, H Gordon Cran, was now made a member of the committee.)

Notes from a meeting held 23 March 1948:
Arising out of the correspondence it was noted that a pension of 20% had been awarded to Mr J Gaunt of Upper Denby as from 27 August 1947. Mr Gaunt's letter of thanks to the committee was also read.

Notes from a meeting held 20 April 1948:
With reference to the War Memorial to those who fell during the 1939-45 War the following arrangements are provisionally arranged.

J W Rowley moved and W Bedford seconded that the ceremony be on Sunday 20 June 1948.

J Thackra moved that Mr N Turton get in touch with the Rev. J Briggs for him to dedicate the Memorial.

G Owen moved that Mr H G Cran be asked to unveil the Memorial.

W Kenyon moved that a person who had served in the present war be asked to unveil the Memorial.

A further amendment was proposed by J W Rowley, that the President, Dr Mitchell be invited to unveil the same.

Upon being put to the vote this amendment was carried unanimously.

The Secretary was also instructed to write to the Denby Dale Silver Prize Band asking them for their services and also the use of the Band Room for the starting and finishing point of the parade.

G Owen moved that we ask our [ex] President H G Cran and E Goldthorpe Esq. President of the West Riding County British Legion to take the salute and this was carried.

Proposed by G Owen that Mr Sykes Wood be in command of the parade.

Denby Dale War Memorial, flanked by the Wesleyan Methodist Church and the Victoria Memorial Hall. Circa 1930.

The Denby Dale War Memorial in its garden setting. Circa 1920.

Notes from a meeting held 4 May 1948:
A letter was received from H G Cran, [ex] President of the Branch regretting that he would be unable to attend the ceremony and also take the salute after the service

Members of The Denby Dale Branch of the British Legion
1 October 1950- 30 September 1951

The following now includes veterans of the Second World War alongside veterans of the First World War:

Dr D E Mitchell	Fred Fish	Jack Lockwood
H G Cran (Life Member)	Robert Fallowfield	Colin Lodge
H Netherwood	Alfred George	Arthur Littlewood
J G Freeman	Wilfred Green	Frank Littlewood
A F F Hall	Harry Green	Haydn Law
W Kenyon	Wilson Green	Arthur Lodge
J Kitson (Life Member)	Thomas Glover	Reg Lawton
Rev. G Barrow	John Gaunt	Eric Littlewood
Rufus Armitage	Ralph Greaves	Walter Lockwood
Kenneth Brook	A Greensmith	Ronald Morgan
John Blacker	Gilbert Goodman	Frank Marsden
Sydney Blackburn	Mr Hamilton	Jack Marsden
Henry Blackburn	Jack Heath	Ralph Morton
George Bower	Desmond Heath	Wilburt Morris
Fred Bower (aged over 65)	Jack Horsley	Frank Morris
Arthur E Brown	Clifford Horsley	Milton Morris
Walter Brown	John W Haigh	George Mallinson
Bernard Broadbent	Norman Haigh	Harvey Mitchell
Ben Blacker	Bobbie Haigh	Stanley Micklethwaite
George D Blacker	Noel Haigh	Cyril Maude
Thomas H Bridge	Walter Holmes	Frank Maude
George A Bostwick	Derek Holmes	Reg Morley
Wilfred Bailey	Fred Hirst	George Mumford
Alfred W Bedford	Jack Hirst	James Murray
Ernest W Burdett	George W Hirst	Stewart Noble
Harold Burdett	Robert Hirst	Brian Noble
Milton Beever	Reg Hudson	Harold Nelson
Lawrence Beaumont	George Hudson	Ronald Newsome
George Barton	W G Hallas	George Owen

Frank Barraclough
James R Barber
Roy Cariledge
Thomas Charlesworth
Kenneth Craven
Archie Craven
Fred Chilton
Ben Coldwell
Roy Crossland
Ronald Craven
Denis Clegg
Denis Coppin
James Clay
Bernard Cunningham
Robert Chilton
Willie Cunningham
Edward Davies
Joseph England
Raymond Ellery
Stanley Fish
Winifred Firth (Adamski)
Herbert Firth (aged over 65)
Herbert Firth
Albert Firth
Thomas Fretwell
Fred K Fisher
Bernard Fisher
Reg Frankland
Roy Frankland
Wilfred Fisher
William Shaw
Denis Shaw
Denis Stephenson
William Swain
George Stott
Harry Schofield
Raymond Sutcliffe
Selwyn Simpson
George Simminds
Joe W Schofield

Cecil Hallas
Clarence Heeley
James B Hargrave
Cecil Hargrave
Donald Hardy
Phyllis Hardy
Percy Hodgson
Geoffrey Horn
Ronnie Hey
Watson Hellewell
Frank Hobson
J Heeley
Kenneth Hughes
Richard Kendal
Clarence Ibbotson
Eric Kenyon
William Kenyon
J R Kenyon
Herbert Kilner
Moorhouse Kaye
Harold Kaye
Frank Kendal
Wilfred Lawton
Harry Lawton
Eric Lockwood
Claude Lockwood
Arthur Lockwood
Wilfred Lockwood
Roy Lockwood
Fred Lockwood
Jack Turner
Eric Turner
Cyril Tingay
Cecil Tingay
Norman Turton
Harold Turton (of Denby)
Harold Turton (of Denby)
Thomas Thackra
William Taylor
George Taylor

George Priest
Willie Pell
Gilbert Pell
Vincent Peace
Thomas Peace
Alex Peace
Fred Peace
Harold Peace
James H Pell
Gordon Robinson
John W Rowley
Clifford Rowley
Clarence Rowley
Charles Ryan
Leonard Robinson
Donald Robinson
George Rhodes
Edward Riggott
George Radley
Desmond Roebuck
John W Senior
Douglas Senior
George Senior
Brian Senior
Arthur Smith
Ernest Smith
Gilbert Smith
Kenneth Smith
Roy Smith
Leslie Shaw
Stanley Whitlam
Sam Wood
Sykes Wood
Ronald Wood
WilliamWoffinden
W J S Whittle
Gilbert Wright
Norman Wadsworth
William Wade
Thomas Wilkinson

D Sharpe	Arthur Tinsley (aged over 65)	John Ward
Derick Smith	Walter Turton (aged over 65)	Leonard Woodhead Geoffrey Thorpe
Frank Tann	Frank Whitehead	
John W Thorpe	Lewis Tarbatt	
Tom Turner	Granville Tucker	

The Royal Air Force Benevolent Fund.

PATRON: H.M. THE KING.
PRESIDENT: H.R.H. THE DUCHESS OF KENT.
CHAIRMAN: THE RT. HON. LORD RIVERDALE, G.B.E.

Telephone No.: LANGHAM 8343/9.
All Communications to be addressed to the Secretary.

67, PORTLAND PLACE,
LONDON, W.1.

Our Reference WJC/MIS/BOX/2 HR.
Your Reference

24th April 1950.

The Hon. Secretary,
British Legion Service Committee,
Kitchenroyd,
Denby Dale,
Huddersfield.

Dear Sir,

In reply to your letter of the 20th inst., we shall be very glad to consider assisting the ex-RAF., man concerned and in order that we may be in possession of the usual details I am enclosing one of our official forms. Would you kindly arrange for this to be completed in detail and returned at your early convenience.

When replying, would you kindly inform me whether there are any outstanding debts as you will appreciate that we cannot supplement National Assistance beyond the usual rate of 10/- per week and it is felt desirable that every advantage should be taken of help from official sources.

I understand the reason why some people are still very reluctant to approach the N.A.B., for help in times of need, but it should be impressed upon them that this is now a right, in view of the increased weekly contributions to N.H.I.

Awaiting the favour of an early reply and thanking you for your most helpful co-operation.

Yours truly,

(W. J. Chandler),
for Wing Commander,
Deputy Secretary.

PLEASE QUOTE OUR REFERENCE NUMBER AT ALL TIMES.

A reply received by the Denby Dale British Legion from the RAF Benevolent Fund regarding financial assistance to one of its veterans, dated April 1950.

Notes from a meeting held 8 January 1954:
Mr L Tarbatt was in the chair and the following members were present: H Firth, W Bailey, F Fisher, R Hudson, J Murray, D Stephenson.

Next meeting Thursday 21 January 1954. Signed Herbert Firth (Chairman).

Notes from a meeting held 17 June 1954:
A letter from the Clerk of the Denby Dale Urban District Council, regarding the Civic Society (4 July) was read out and it was resolved that as many members as possible attend the parade and service at Denby Parish church that day.

Notes from a meeting held 5 August 1954:
That the action of Mr Firth in arranging convalescence at Lowestoft for Mr F Marsden be confirmed was carried. With reference to Mr F Burdett of High Flatts it was agreed that Mr Burdett be asked to see Dr Mitchell regarding his medical report.

Notes from AGM held 9 December 1954:
The President (J Kitson) was re-elected for the year 1955. The Vice-Presidents (with the exception of Mr W V Wade) were re-elected en bloc, *namely: H G Green, H S Netherwood, Dr D E Mitchell, A F Hall, J J Freeman, W Kenyon, G Owen, H Firth, S Wood, J W Rowley, J W Whittle, G Senior, F Hirst.*
Secretary – M Kaye, Treasurer – H Firth, Pensions – H Firth, Chairman – L Tarbatt, Vice-Chairman – F Fisher.
Committee – R Hirst, J Thackra, J Gaunt, D Stephenson, E Smith, R Hudson, W Bailey, R Greaves, G Bower, D Smith.
Standard Bearer – R Hirst.

Over the course of 1955, the minutes make note of attempts to begin a women's section of the Legion. By 1956, this had been established. It is currently unknown how many of the members' wives had become involved, but they had begun taking responsibility for certain elements of fund-raising events, such as whist drives and dances.

Notes from a meeting held 28 July 1955:
Mr Firth reported that Frank Marsden had been successful in getting convalescence at Lowestoft. He has promised that if another member of the Branch deserves to go to Lowestoft he would pay the £3 3s fare.

Notes from a meeting held 15 October 1955:
A complaint was made regarding children playing in the Cenotaph grounds at night and H Firth moved and J Thackra seconded that we write to the Clerk of the Denby Dale Urban District Council asking them to take the matter up with the local police.

Notes from a meeting held 26 January 1956:
Agreed that the Ambulance Room for the children's party be paid for by the men's section.

Regarding outing for this year, it was decided that we go to Blackpool on the 16 of June and that we book three buses provisionally.

Notes from a meeting held 23 February 1956:
That a grant from the Huddersfield War Fund of £1 10s 6d for two weeks be made to Mr Alfred George.

Notes from a meeting held 2 October 1956:
Letters accepting engagement for Children's Party were read from Mr Victor Senior (Magician) and Mr Dennis Lockwood (Puppet Show). A vote that Mr Victor Senior be booked was noted. It was agreed to pass these letters on to the ladies section for their satisfaction.

Notes from AGM held 4 December 1956:
The Chairman thanked all members of the committee for their work during the past year and appealed for young men who have done their National Service to join the British Legion and take an active part in the work of the Local Branch.

Notes from a meeting held 1 January 1957:
With reference to a further whist drive and dance at Denby, the Rev. Moore offered one of their dances, namely 16 July, provided we have the dance band engaged by them and it was decided to accept the offer.

Notes from a meeting held 2 April 1957:
Whist Drives. A satisfactory report was made by Mr G Owen and gratitude was felt for him in his uneasy task over the last few weeks but no definite arrangements could be made for a regular steward.

Notes from a meeting held 16 April 1957:
It was proposed that whist drives in the band room be suspended from 17 April 1957 owing to certain difficulties which had arisen.

These lists are only snapshots of the members during this time, names come and go with relocation and death being the primary causes and new members being recruited all the time.

The Legion in Denby Dale made regular payments to the Lord Kitchener Memorial Home in Lowestoft through the years, and not inconsiderable sums. For instance, in July 1954 they remitted £3 3s. Lord Kitchener died in 1916 when the cruiser *Hampshire* was sunk *en route* to Russia. His death prompted many memorials and the establishment of the home in Lowestoft was one of these. It was initiated by Rev F W Emms as a holiday home for convalescent ex-servicemen. It opened in 1919 and still operates to the present day.

The Denby Dale branch of the Legion was still operating in 1967, as paperwork relating to it has survived, though the date of and reason for its closure are currently unknown. An enquiry to the headquarters of the British Legion in 2016 was answered with the fact that they did not know there had ever been a Denby Dale branch.

Finding ex-members has proved challenging, though not totally impossible, and although the final days of the institution are currently elusive, it is interesting to make a short note of the recollections of one of its former members. Cecil Hallas can be found in the previously mentioned lists and was living at Dry Hill, Lower Denby, when the Second World War broke out. He left school aged 14 and went to work for George Ashworth's hairdressers on Penistone High Street from 1942. He can remember convoys of wagons and Jeeps with large white stars on their sides driving along the main Penistone High Street after the Americans joined the war in December 1941, though the first troops did not arrive until 1942.

Advanced Ammunition Parks used by the RAF were often enlarged to include USAAF munitions. These dumps, which often exploited natural cave systems or dense woodland, used concrete structures as a means of protection. Wortley Hall was requisitioned by the RAF as the headquarters and gave its name to the actual site at Scout Dike near Ingbirchworth. Some US Officers were initially billeted here, though the munitions store stretched from Grenoside to Shepley. Scout Dike was the main accommodation site for troops, though in late 1943, the whole operational HQ was transferred here. The Scout Dike site was fully commissioned by the RAF in April 1942 and it began its transfer to US forces in July 1942, and was fully adopted by the US Ordnance Corps in October 1942. A handover to the US 8th Air Force took place in July 1943, its official name being Ordnance Depot 0-695 Wortley, though it was better known as a reserve ammunition dump.

Cecil Hallas also remembers the first American coming in to the hairdressers, the first American he'd seen up close and asking for an unusual haircut – not the usual 'short back and sides' – and showing him the welt marks across the palms of his hands from working with the ropes as a cowboy in Texas.

"As a lad of about 14, 15, I couldn't believe this – having a cowboy in the shop in Penistone – it was totally out of this world."

Upper Denby Club

The village club was sited upon what is today's green. It is likely that it once occupied a long low building, which is thought to have once belonged to the Moore family, who were the monumental masons in the village. It was perhaps established by the locals due to the success of the one that had opened on Norman Road in Denby Dale. Thomas Norton had undertaken the official opening ceremony here on Saturday 29 September 1894 and was presented with an ornate engraved key for his trouble. It is not known whether the Upper Denby Club had such an auspicious local dignitary for their opening day.

A ceremonial key presented to Thomas Norton of Bagden Hall upon his official opening of Denby Dale Club on Saturday 29 September 1894.

The reverse side of the key. Note the initials T N laid into the enamel.

Details concerning the club are sketchy at best. A billiard table was acquired, which was later removed to the band hut on Gunthwaite Lane, and card-playing was popular along with whist drives. It is unlikely the club ever sold alcohol. Members were required to pay a subscription of 9s per year in monthly instalments, though there were always some members in arrears. The only known surviving details concern the period 1924 – 1928:

Members in 1924		
R Barber	R Beever	N Charlesworth
J Haigh	S Whitlam	H Broadhead
S Broadhead	H White	J Waldie
A Smithson	A Ward	A Broadhead
C H Turton	J Turton	W Gaunt
W Moorhouse	J Kilner	A Rhodes
W Dronfield	E Heath	C H Rotherford
G Dronfield	W Turton	C K Hanwell
J H Gaunt	E Hudson	K Windle
H Garret	A Moorhouse	G Senior
F Widdowson	E Beever	J Kitson
J W White	J Nicholson	F Gaunt
W Mosley	F Lawton	W Windle
A Lockwood	C Beever	

Meetings were held monthly, though to date only one sheet of the minutes taken has survived. This details the following:

Friday 28 September 1928. R Beevor – Secretary, C H Turton – Treasurer.

Monday 5 October 1928. Committee – J Turton, F Rusby, E Beevor, W Todhunter, K Windle, C Broad, J W White, E Heath, L Windle, C H Turton, J Turton, N White, J Haigh. Entrance fee set at 1s 6d. Committee meeting Friday 6 October 1928 – meetings to be held once a month after.

Proposed by C H Turton, seconded by J Turton that all-four card games be played until one party gets 21.

Proposed by C H Turton seconded by J W White that there shall be no gambling in the club and all members not adhering to the rule shall be expelled.

Whist Drive and Dance 8 December 1928.
MC for Whist – J H Gaunt, MC for Dance – C Broad.

Proposed by C H Turton, seconded by J Haigh that the Secretary writes and engages the Manhattan Dance Band for dance on 8 December 1928.

Proposed by C H Turton, seconded by J W White that the Secretary gets 25 Crown folio bills for dance.

A page from Upper Denby Club subscriptions list and payments for 1924.

> *Proposed by N White, seconded by C Broad, that all card games must be paid for by the loser.*

> *Proposed C H Turton, seconded by C Broad, that the club must be locked up every night at 10:30pm.*

> *Proposed by J W White, seconded by B Beevor, that the club closes at 10:00pm on Sunday nights.*

> *Proposed by C H Turton that the Secretary places card rules in the card room.*

It would seem from the latter that this document details the founding of the village club. Further whist drives and dances were held in 1927 and 1928, and money was being raised in 1927 from subscriptions with the aim of building a new clubhouse. From photographs that show the buildings on the triangle, it seems the committee were successful and a newer building was erected and the former clubhouse either sold on or rented out to James (Jimmy Pump) Gaunt.

The club's bank balance for 1927 was £10 14s 9d. Further subscriptions raised £5 16s 0d through the autumn, and winter's total was £4 18s 9d. The subscriptions ledger ends abruptly in February 1928, detailing more money raised. The book is far from completed but the reason for its cessation is unknown. The buildings on the village green were demolished between 1957 and 1962, though it is likely that the club had disbanded some considerable time before this, which was probably when the billiard table made its way up to the band hut.

The Senior Family of Denby Dale

As previously made clear, my dad was the main reason I became interested in local history, but there was one other source of encouragement and that was from a very special individual. Not only did he make a teenager welcome in his house and share information, it was also he that first suggested I write a book. He lived long enough to see the first two in print and was positive about their content. His name was William Herbert Senior, Herbert to his friends.

Herbert was born in Denby Dale into a family that could trace its roots in the village (and Cumberworth) back until at least the eighteenth century and most likely much further. He was related to the founding father of Kenyons Mills and was also the village's very knowledgeable local historian. Herbert was born in 1905, the third child of Charlie and Elizabeth Senior. His working life was spent at the textile firm Edward Blackburn based in Scissett, where he eventually became a director. He was a member of the 1928 Denby Dale pie committee and in his younger days helped to run a variety of societies that included a football team and a gramophone club. He also became the chief ARP warden for the Denby Dale area during the Second World War.

It was Herbert's passion for history, particularly Yorkshire and local history, that was to set him apart. He had no formal qualifications in the subject or, for that matter, as a teacher. But he was passionate about his interest and was a gifted communicator. In 1963, he began running evening classes for the old West Riding Education Authority, and these continued under Kirklees in Holmfirth and Shelley. He also taught with the Workers Educational Association in Leeds and Barnsley, and was a founder tutor with the Huddersfield branch of the University of the Third Age. In 1997, he founded a new class, The Yorkshire Studies Group, which was based at Shepley and so popular that it could soon boast of over a hundred members. His talks would not only include history, they would vary from music to mythology or even his travels abroad, and all would be illustrated by his slide collection, which ran into the tens of thousands. Indeed, my own introduction to Herbert was being taken to one of his illustrated lectures at Upper Denby Church by my father. Herbert was also filmed at home by BBC *Look North* during 1988 for a programme made about the Denby Dale pie of that year.

In 2000, he was awarded an MBE for his services to education and local history and travelled to Buckingham Palace in June to receive it from the queen. After shaking his hand the queen remarked: "Your subject is a fascinating one and Yorkshire is a most interesting county."

He was also one of the guests of honour at the 2000 Denby Dale pie celebrations in September that year. Later that month, and in his 95th year, Herbert died. But he left behind many friends and a legacy as important as any historian of the past. As this branch of the Senior family tree has never been published before, it is a pleasure to include it now along with photographs of the family.

Herbert's lineage currently begins with the birth of Joseph Senior in Denby Dale/Cumberworth in 1762. He married Elizabeth Wood in 1785, who was very possibly a relative of John Wood (1755-1831), the man responsible for bringing Wesleyan Methodism to Denby Dale.

Senior Family 1

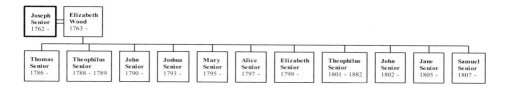

The above-named Joshua Senior married Elizabeth Longley (born 1794) in 1822 and had the following children: Martha (born 1823), Alice (born 1824), John (born 1826), William (born 1828), Hannah (born 1830), Eliza (Born 1832), Joshua (born 1834), William (born 1835) and Charles (born 1837).

Theophilus Senior was born in 1801 and was baptised at the Wesleyan Methodist chapel in Denby Dale. Later he can be found living at Cliffe Style in Silkstone in the 1841 census. He married Elizabeth Burdett, no doubt a relative of the old lords of the manor of Denby, and they had at least twelve children. By the time of the 1841 census, Theophilus and his family were back in Denby Dale where he was working as a fancy weaver and, by 1851, his occupation was described as a silk and worsted hand-loom weaver. By 1871, he was described as a widower and so Elizabeth (born 1803) had died. He was still recorded as a fancy weaver.

Senior Family 2

Martha Senior married Francis Loughead (born 1825) and had the following children: Matilda (b.1845), Wilson (b.1846), Kate (b.1848), Jane (b.1850), Mary Ann (b.1852), Laura (b.1856), Clara (b.1862), Edith (b.1864), William (b.1867), Gertrude (b.1869).

Joseph Senior married Martha Brook (b.1831) and had the following children: James (b.1851), Arthur (b.1854), Mary (b.1860), Margaret (b.1864), Edward (b.1868) and Joseph (b. 1873).

Ann Senior married John Appleyard (b.1820) and had Tedbar (b.1851) and Charles (b.1854).

Eliza married Edwin Heeley (1831-1863) and had Norris (b.1860) and Joe (b.1863).

Hannah married William Eastwood (b.1838) and had the following children: Arthur (b.1862), Samuel (b.1866), Ada (b.1868), Mary (b.1870), Alice (b.1874), Carrie (b.1876) and Harry (b.1880).

William married Emma Bradshaw/Mary Wortley.

George married Mary Wortley.

The line continues from Theophilus to his son Thomas, also baptised at the Wesleyan Methodist Chapel in Denby Dale in 1830. Like his father, Thomas also became a fancy weaver. He married Ellen Haigh in 1853 and had at least seven children. The family lived on School Terrace in Denby Dale, though by the time of the 1881 census, only Mary, Hannah, Clara and Charlie were still at the family home.

Senior Family 3

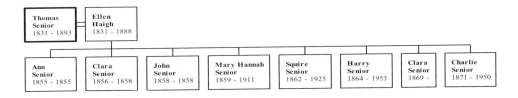

Squire Senior married Elizabeth Hirst (b.1862) in 1883 and had: Bertha (b.1884), Polly (b.1886), Ellen (b.1889), George (b.1892), Maggie (b.1893), Annie (b.1895), Joe (b.1899) and Arthy (b.1900).

Harry Senior married Mary Ellen (b.1864) and had: Wilfred (b.1889), Lillie (b.1890), Elsie (b.1894), Thomas (b.1896), Agnes (b.1898) and Annie (b.1900).

Clara married Arthur Firth.

Thomas was recorded as a fancy woollen weaver in 1881 and a cotton warp dresser in 1891, though he died two years later aged 62. His son Charlie can be found in the 1891 census, aged 19, working as a power loom tuner. This had altered little by 1901, when he was recorded as a worsted power loom tuner. He married Elizabeth Firth in 1896 and had three children, the above-mentioned William Herbert, Florence and Charles Haydn, known as Haydn Senior. It was Haydn's marriage to Margaret Kenyon that brought the link to the mill-owning clan into the Senior family. Margaret Kenyon's father was Thomas Herbert Kenyon, who was in turn the son of John Kenyon, who was the son of Jonas Kenyon, who founded Dearneside Mills in 1854.

Thomas Senior (1831-1893) father of Charlie and grandfather of William

Jonathan Crossland, seated with his wife Ann (formerly Hanwell), with children Ellen (b.1877), and Hannah (b.1884) sitting on the stool, taken around 1890.

Left to right: John Kenyon (1846-1903) seated, stroking the dog, behind him is probably his second wife Jane Morley, who he married in 1884. Eva Wood Kenyon and Mary Ann Kenyon – John's mother (seated). The other woman may have been Sarah Morley, sister of Jane. Circa 1890.

John Kenyon (1846-1903) taken circa the late 1870s.

This photograph was marked on the back 'Mrs Crossland'. It is presumably Jonathan's wife Ann Hanwell in later life, probably taken just before the First World War.

135

Left to right, standing: Sarah Morley (probably), Eva Wood Kenyon. Seated: Jane Morley, John Kenyon and Mary Ann Kenyon, around 1900.

Thomas Herbert Kenyon (1872-1913), son of John and Harriet Kenyon, taken around 1895.

Martha Elizabeth Kenyon (Aunt Lizzie, b.1862), sister of John Kenyon, taken at Christmas 1914.

Ellen (Nellie) Crossland (1877-1955), daughter of Jonathan and Ann Crossland, taken around the late 1890s.

A ladies' ramble in the woods taken somewhere close to Denby Dale. The picture was developed by the village photographers Hanson & Turton. Ellen (Nellie) Crossland is seated to the bottom right. Circa 1905.

Ellen (Nellie) Crossland with her eldest child John, who was baptised in 1909.

An older Thomas Herbert Kenyon with his eldest child, John, probably on his christening day in 1909.

A studio portrait of a group wearing their country finery. Thomas Herbert Kenyon is third from the left at the back.

Eva Wood Kenyon, daughter of John and Harriet Kenyon, taken just prior to the onset of the First World War.

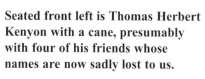

Seated front left is Thomas Herbert Kenyon with a cane, presumably with four of his friends whose names are now sadly lost to us.

Charlie and Elizabeth Senior with their children standing behind them, left to right: Florence (Florrie), Charles Haydn and William Herbert, probably taken around 1914

Charlie and Elizabeth's three children, left to right: Florence (Florrie), William Herbert and Charles Haydn.

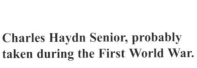

Charlie Senior with his sons, William Herbert and Charles Haydn, taken during the early 1920s.

Charles Haydn Senior, probably taken during the First World War.

Group portrait of the wedding of Charles Haydn Senior and Margaret Kenyon on 1 August 1936 at Denby Dale. Back row left to right: Thomas Blamires, William Herbert Senior, ?, Charles Haydn Senior, Margaret Kenyon, John Kenyon (Margaret's brother), Charlie Senior. Seated left to right: Elizabeth Senior (Charlie's wife), the bridesmaids were Nellie Cooper and Kathleen Turton although it is not known which is which, Ellen (Nellie) Kenyon.

Charlie Senior (right) playing bowls at the green at Heywood Bottom, Denby Dale. Circa 1930s.

William Herbert Senior in about 1925.

Denby Dale Bowling Club members pose with a trophy that can be identified from the poster in the clubhouse window. It is the T A Hinchliffe Cup. Thomas Albert Hinchliffe (1864-1922), the son of mill owner Zaccheus Hinchliffe, was instrumental in obtaining the land for both the bowling and cricket clubs in the village. Charlie Senior can be seen on the first left of the middle row. Circa 1930s.

William Herbert Senior receiving his MBE from Queen Elizabeth II at Buckingham Palace in 2000.

William Herbert Senior with his MBE in 2000.

141

Senior Family 4

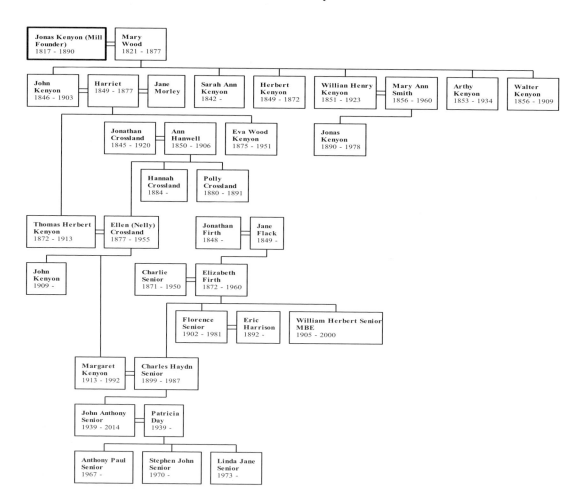

The above-mentioned Kenyon family tree is not included in full, please see *Denby & District II* for the complete table.

AUGUST, 1927. PRICE 2d.

OUR JOINT
Parish . Magazine.

S. Aidan's Skelmanthorpe.
Vicar—The Rev E. Teale, B.A., M.C. J.P.
Churchwardens—Messrs. C. H. Taylor* and E. Ellis.
Sidesmen—Messrs H. Haigh, A. T. Last, O. Peel, A. Peel, J. Field, H. Dickinson A. Mallinson, J. Exley.
Church Council—The Vicar & Wardens, Messrs. H. Haigh, A. T. Last. O. Peel, A. Peel, J. Exley, W. Ladkin, A Mallinson, H. Mann, J. A. Buttery, H. Dickinson, A. Briddock, T. Gawthorpe, Mesdames M. Fisher, A. Jebson, H. L. Taylor, T. W. Senior, S. A. Hinchliffe, Miss E. Senior.
Verger—Mr. A. Briddock, Smithy Lane.

S. Augustine's, Scissett.
Vicar—The Rev. H. C. Libbey, B.Sc.
Churchwardens—Messrs. F. Ashton and L. H. Hardcastle.
Sidesmen—Messrs. T, H. Batty, E. Beaumont, T. Beaumont, A. Craven, B. Dickinson, W. Firth, N. Fisher, A. Hardcastle, W. Hardcastle, G. T. Hellewell, F.Leake, J. Pell, C. Shaw, J. Wilkinson, A. Wood, A. Woodhead.
Church Council—Messrs. R. J. H. Beanland, * E. Beaumont, H. Bates. W. Green, A. Hardcastle, T. Morley, G. H. Norton,* H. B. Peace. B. B. Shaw, A. Wood, Mrs. Beanland, Miss M. H. Craven, Miss Eva Exley, Miss A, Green, Mrs. Libbey, Miss Norton.
Verger—Mr. A. Craven, Stanhope Street

S. John the Evangelist's Denby.
Vicar— The Rev. G. O. Tibbits, L.Th., Dur.
Churchwardens—Messrs. A. Jelfs, and T. W. Senior.
Sidesmen—Messrs. J. R. Waldie, T. Rusby, G. Rotherforth, J. H. Hanwell, N. Charlesworth, H. N. Naylor, G. Shaw, H. Hudson, F. Widdowson, R. A. Smithson. Joe Turton and J. Waldie.
Church Council—The Vicar and Wardens, Messrs. J. R. Waldie*, T. Rusby, G. Rotherforth. R. Barber, Mesdames T. W. Senior, T. Rusby, Misses Hinchliffe, Walters, Nicholson and Tibbits.
Verger—Mr. R. Barber.

S. Nicholas' Church, Cumberworth
Rector—Rev W. A. Taylor, M A., Hon C.F.
Churchwardens—Messrs. W. H. Tarbatt and G. Benson.
Sidesmen—Messrs. E. Benson. W. Smith, Wm. Peace, W. Rollinson. G. H. Hanwell, L. Hollingworth, N. Dearnley, G. H. Turton, J.H. Fretwell L. Benson, J. H. Swift, W. Schofield, H. Walker, Frank Firth, D. Birkett.
Church Council—The Rector and Wardens, Mrs. Goodall, Mrs. A. Shaw, Mrs. W. Peace. Mrs. Walker, Mrs. Cran,* Misses B. Turton, C Hollingworth and D. Smith. Messrs. J. Hollingworth J. H. Fretwell, W. Smith, E. Benson, and Mrs. W. A. Taylor (Co-opted.)
Sexton—Mr. L. Mellor, The Old Rectory.

Emmanuel Church, Shelley.
Vicar—Rev. A. T. Walkden, M.A., Hon. C.F.
Churchwardens—Messrs. A. W. Ramsden* and R. Jaggar.*
Sidesmen—Messrs. A. Armitage, W. Addy, W. Brunt, A. Chadwick, W. Earnshaw, G. E. Hall, W. Hanson, H. Holbrook Walter Hanson, W. Peatman, F. Shaw.
Church Council—The Vicar & Wardens, Messrs. A. Armitage, W. Hanson, H. Hanson, G. P. Norton, R. Sykes, Mesdames H. Brook, M. Brunt. A. Haigh, E. Marsh, D. Norton, S. A. Kirk, Misses L. Addy, C. Stephenson.
Verger—Mr. G. H. Rollinson, School House.

All Saints', Clayton West
Rector—
Churchwardens—Messrs. W. Sheard and H. Dyson.
Sidesmen—Messrs. E. Marshall, W. Burgess, C. Pinder, J. Barber, F. Exley, G. Haigh, J. Hirst, E. Clarkson
Church Council—The Rector & Wardens, Messrs. P. Addy, (Sec.) F. Hammerton*, J. E. Barber, E. Marshall, L. Haigh, J. E. Blacker, W Sheard, J. H. Armitage. Miss Wintour. Miss Holmes, Miss Naylor, Miss Drake, Mrs Dyson
Caretaker—Mrs Armitage, Chapel Hill.

S Paul's Church, Shepley
Vicar - The Rev. B. G. D. Clarke, M.A.
Churchwardens—Messrs. B. S. Armitage and A. W. Stephenson
Sidesmen Messrs. P. Addy, J. E. Ellis, W. Fulton, W. H. Haigh, W. Haigh, (Jun.), Wilson Smith, W. Stephenson, A. Stewart. T. J. Thorpe, A. Townend, W. G. Wadsworth and G. Webster.
Church Council—The Vicar and Wardens, Mesdames B. G. D. Clarke, E. Pearson, B. H. Roberts, J. Smith, Misses H. Noble, C. Noble, M. Washington, R. Wood, F. Wortley, Messrs P. Addy, J. Armitage, J. E. Ellis, W. H Haigh, W. Hey, L. Mosley. W. Reeds, Wilson Smith*, H. Sunderland, J. Thorpe, A. Townend, W. G. Wadsworth, (Hon. Sec.), G. Washington. G. Webster.
Verger & Caretaker—Mr. H. Morton, School House

Holy Trinity Church, Denby Dale.
Priest-in-Charge—Rev. M. MacColl.
Churchwardens—Messrs. A. Kenyon* & R. Hobson.
Sidesmen—Messrs. A. Atkin, J. Bridge, G. H. Brook,W. Dyson, A. V. Ellis, P Howard, Ernest, Walter, Fred & Frank Littlewood. B. Ackroyd, E. Hobson
Church Council—Misses F. Bransgrove, (Hon. Sec.,) M. Howard, Messrs. A. Kenyon, J. Bridge, G. H. Brook, A. V. Ellis, E. Lockwood R. Hobson, Mrs. Pitcher.
Caretaker—Mr. E. Hartley, Morley Bottom
Members of the Church Councils marked * are also Representatives to the Diocesan Conference.

HIRST BUCKLEY, PRINTER, SCISSETT.

It is unknown how long the local parishes produced a joint magazine; this is the front cover of the only copy to have come to light so far.

S. AIDAN'S.

We are very grateful to Canon Smith for his talks to us at the Morning and Evening Services on our Anniversary Sunday. No one could possibly feel that they were preached at. What they would feel would be that they were talked to; talked to, or talked with, about very important things in an encouraging sort of way. I am not going to analyze all he said. I should be overrating my ability if I made an attempt of that kind. And I should be spoiling the impression Canon Smith made. His story of Old Jane was delightful. Old Jane was a character, that is the expression we use of anyone who is out standing. Old Jane stood out above the rest who lived in the same street. She had no use for Parsons. There are a number of people like that nowadays, but not in Jane's way. She slammed the door against them whenever they called; not vindictively, nor with any obvious feeling of resentment. Just slammed, that is all. But one night she was ill. She was in pain, and in the midst of her discomfort and loneliness she made a pact with God. Jane was not irreverent. She prayed that if God would send her a drop o' gin she would let the Parson come in and talk with her the next time he called. Soon after, the door opened, a neighbour came in and said, "Jane, ah've brought yer a drop o' gin. Ah thought mebbe yer'd like it, and it 'ud do yer good". Jane kept her word. She let the Parson in the next time he called. "Yer can come in now and talk to me" she said. Ever afterwards Jane became a ministering angel to the people round about; people whose lives were hard, but who were responsive to Jane's thoughtful consideration, and many acts of simple kindliness. Canon Smith emphasized the point that while we are learning to pray we should pray for the things we know we want; the things on the common level of daily experience. Later on we shall be led to pray for the things God wants us to want (I can only put it that way) because we shall have learnt to want them too.

The story of Jane is a true story. It was not an illustration manufactured by Canon Smith to emphasize a point in his address. I wish I'd known Jane. Canon Smith thought I had known her, but he was mistaken. If I had known her there would be the memory permanently imbedded in my mind of a personality sent by God for the purpose of inspiring and encouraging ordinary folk. Most of us are very ordinary folk who need inspiring now and again in our colourless lives, and a lot of encouragement. There may be differences amongst us which are very deeply and vividly outlined. Some of us by the mysterious chances and accidents of life may have all that life can give. Some of us may be faced with unending struggles, and with anxieties which never seem to cease. These differences make life very artificial, and incline us to emphasize wrong values, but when we come down to the essential art of living we are all very ordinary folk; folk who need a lot of encouragement now and again, simple consideration and understanding, and the smiles and greetings of our friends. It is a pity there are not more Janes in our midst; a pity that we do not know what we really want.

GARDEN PARTY, Tuesday, August 2nd. Arrangements are being made for a Garden Party in the Vicarage grounds on the evening of this date. It will not be a big affair for the simple reason that the Vicarage garden is not a big one, nor is it wondrously beautiful as many of the gardens one hears and reads about. The Garden Party may not be very ably organized; there may not be cocoa-nut shies, nor intriguing side shows, nor handsome bandsmen deliciously uniformed to play to us; there may be no music at all, but that does not matter really. What we want is just to meet each other over a cup of tea at about half past five or six o'clock, play a few games on the lawn, and talk to each other friendly like. If you care to join us we feel sure you will enjoy your evening. We want good weather, a warm summer's evening on that day, and I wish to goodness that American hadn't prophesied an Artic Summer in these Northern latitudes, because it makes everything so uncertain, and us a bit frightened.

A Change. Mr. Maurice Buckley who has been our organist for a little while leaves us at the end of this month for Scissett Parish Church. This is rather a blow, and a surprise to us. We really had thought that Maurice was one of us, and we cannot help feeling very sorry that he has taken up this other appointment. There are excellent personal reasons why he should go to Scissett, and one quite readily understands. The decision must have been a difficult one for him to make. We wish him every success in his new work, and we hope he will be as happy there as he has been with us. We know what his capabilities are, and what an excellent organist he will become.

In Maurice's place we have appointed Mr. George Walker of Clayton West. Mr. Walker comes to us with excellent references, and from what we know of him we feel sure we shall get on extremely well together. He will find that we are very friendly people, and very appreciative of all that he might do for us. He will be admirably suited with our organ, one knows that; we hope he will like us and be happy in his work amongst us.

The Skelmanthorpe page.

S. AUGUSTINE'S.

HOLY BAPTISM.

July 10   Joan Margaret, daughter of Irvine and Norah Green.

July 17   Joan, daughter of Ernest and Elsie Gertrude Atkinson.

HYMNS FOR THE MONTH.

Aug. 7 M: 150 460 461
       E: 360 300 179
  14 M: 3 243 548 517
      E: 390 356 477
  21 3 p.m. 520 512   19
  28 M: 242 531 623 600
      E: 452 454 588

SCISSETT VICARAGE,
July, 1927.

My dear People,

The Magazine has a somewhat wider range than the pulpit, and I may therefore be permitted here to indulge in a privilege some of my readers do not afford to me on a Sunday. Of course, preaching is by no stretch of imagination the chief part of the Service. I think it is the least part, and if by any chance it were to be a 'draw' I should have serious doubts as to the sincerity of the worship. One thing, however, is certain; those of you who make a regular practice of withholding yourselves from the House of God are making a very grave mistake. And if there be any who turn aside from religion and suppose that a social gospel will remedy the evils which they encounter, they are making a still graver mistake, and are cherishing an empty illusion. This world will never be set right without both the Person and the Principles of Christ enthroned at the heart of things. The House of God is the place where men and women endeavour to honour Him and to learn what is His Will. I can only, in the brief space here permitted, beg you to consider how mistaken a course you have been led into; and that both for your own sake and for your children's you will join in corporate worship. There is an old saying, "Judge not a book by the cover". One fears that many judge Christianity by the cover. I know some of us make a poor show, but the Thing itself is priceless. With every hope,

I am,

Your friend and Vicar,

Hubert C. Libbey.

A New Hymn Book ?

With or without the possibility of the new Prayer Book coming into use, the introduction of a new Hymn Book is in our minds. Increasingly throughout the Church THE ENGLISH HYMNAL is finding favour. A fuller and more varied expression will certainly enrich our Services. It will be of some interest to know that just over 70 per cent. of Hymns A. and M. have been in regular use within recent years, which means that the field of this book has been adequately explored. This brief note is merely indicative of a possible change.

The District Nurse.

The Annual Report of the Scissett and District Nursing Association has recently come to hand. It will interest our readers to know that Nurse Sharples, S.R.N., C.M.B., has made 3,093 visits and assisted at 104 cases (Surgical, Medical, etc.) during the year. We are glad to have the opportunity here of testifying to the valuable and capable work Nurse Sharples is constantly doing.

Holiday Week.

August 20—27. May it be a fine sunny week for all concerned! The Scouts hope to spend the week in camp, somewhere. Through the great kindness of neighbouring Clergy the Services on Sunday Aug. 21, will be these : Holy Communion 9-0, Celebrant, the Rector of Cumberworth ; Evensong 3-0, Preacher, the Rector of Emley.

The Organist.

After advertising in a local newspaper for one to succeed the late Mr. Hirst Buckley—whose loss both as a personality and an organist we feel acutely—our choice, after the most careful consideration, fell upon his elder son, Mr. Maurice Buckley. We cannot but feel sorry that a neighbouring Church loses in consequence. To Maurice we extend our cordial welcome, and hope his career with us will be long and happy. Mr. George Wray has willingly stepped into the breach, and we are both greatly indebted and thankful to him for helping us in our need.

The Churchyard.

A wire refuse basket has been procured for the Churchyard. Those who trim the graves are asked to deposit rubbish therein. Its use adequately will probably lead to the provision of another.

The Church Clock.

We hope to be able to write at some length upon this subject next month. The Clock Fund now stands at £55-13-0.

The Scissett page.

Our Joint Parish Magazine.

AUGUST, 1927.

High Hoyland & Clayton West.

WALKER VICARAGE,
July 19th, 1927.

Dear People,

I am looking forward to coming among you at the end of August, encouraged by the promise of your Church Officials of a hearty welcome.

This time of change is a trying one for everyone concerned, and please remember, not least so, for the newcomers. But it has one advantage, and that is, it gives those who perhaps have dropped into slack habits and given up the worship of God in Church, the opportunity to make a new start.

The Collect for Sunday before last reminded us that without God.—"Nothing is strong, nothing is holy". May we all resolve to work together for God's glory, and live in "Unity and Godly Love" and thus bring blessing upon the parish.

Yours sincerely,
N. G. Hounsfield.

Choir.

A most enjoyable day was spent at Ripon by the members of the Choir, on the 16th of July.

The journey was made by road, and as the weather was on its best behaviour, that part of the outing was greatly appreciated. A visit was made during the afternoon to the ruins of Fountains Abbey, and also to the beautiful little Church at Studley. The party arrived home about 11-30 p.m., tired but very pleased with the day's experiences.

We cannot let this opportunity pass without expressing the thanks of all our Churchpeople to the Choir on the admirable way they have kept together during the five months we have been without Rector. It is difficult to carry on, but our Choir have never failed us at any Service, and we do gratefully express our thanks to them.

At Rest.

It is with great regret that we have to record the death of one of our devoted helpers, Mrs. Puddephatt. She was a member of the Mothers' Union, and took an active interest in any work for our Church and Parish. She will be missed, and we extend our heartfelt sympathy to her family in the severe loss they have sustained.

MARRIAGES.

July 7   Samuel Baxter Doyle and Lily Woffindin.
„ 7   Frank Allott and Lena Woffindin.

BURIALS.

May 26   Jane Elizabeth Hill, aged 59 years.
June 9   Elizabeth Foster, aged 64 years.
June 27   Mary Sykes, aged 82 years.
July 19   Walter Shaw, aged 60 years.

The High Hoyland & Clayton West page.

S. NICHOLAS' CHURCH.

CUMBERWORTH RECTORY,

My dear Parishioners,

As many of you are aware Mr. MacColl has asked me to take steps to appoint a successor as soon as possible. It seems a pity that he should leave the Parish after such a short acquaintance as he has already done good work in rallying many of the young people of Denby Dale round the Church, and in attracting a congregation by his gifts as a preacher, so that one wonders what solid work for the Church he might have achieved after a longer stay. However, he feels that he would do better work elsewhere, and so we have no alternative but to let him go. We are very grateful to him for his kindness in offering to remain for a little while, in order to give us the chance of obtaining someone in his place.

Curates do not seem to have stayed very long in this Parish, with the exception of the Rev. G. H. Horton, and perhaps the following list will be of interest to our readers :—

T. N. Rigby	..	1892—1895
H. Lancaster	...	1895—1898
W. G. Cook	...	1898—1899
V. H. Haddelsey	...	1899—1902
G. H. Horton	...	1902—1914
J. F. L. Orton	...	1914—1917
J. S. Walker	...	1918—1923
T. W. Hogarth	...	1923—1926
M. MacColl	...	1926

We are endeavouring to obtain another faithful Priest to take his place in this Apostolic Succession, but this will not be an easy task owing to the great shortage of Clergy at present. Not only are many Curacies vacant throughout the country, but Patrons are finding difficulty even in filling Livings. Before the war about 600 men were being ordained every year. Now the number has fallen to about 300. The reasons for this falling off are largely economic. A College training is more expensive than it used to be, and at the same time, for very good reasons, the Bishops are insisting on a higher intellectual standard than ever before. Again, many of the families which used to provide the candidates for Holy Orders find themselves among the "new poor", and cannot afford to send their sons to College, and the "new rich", who have taken their places, encourage their boys to enter on some career which will bring in more "brass" than being a "parson." However, the Church as a whole is taking the matter up, and specially selected candidates are being assisted at College by Central and Diocesan Funds. There is one very encouraging feature in the outlook, namely that there are plenty of young men who would gladly offer themselves for Holy Orders if they had the wherewithal for their training. The shortage is not in human material, but in financial stringency.

But, to return home, if we are left for a time without Curate, it will mean that I must divide my direct responsibility between the two Churches. Though adequately robust for one person I cannot divide myself into two, so the situation will involve such things as the employment of lay readers, the rearrangement of hours of services, and possibly even the cutting down of some services. If and when this is necessary I hope I may count on the ungrudging help and support of every member of the two congregations, and I appeal to all now to make the future of Church life and work in this Parish a subject of earnest prayer.

Your sincere friend and Rector,

W. A. Taylor.

MOTHERS' UNION.

Unfortunately our visit to Rockwood arranged for July 6th, had to be postponed owing to Mrs. Cran's illness. An ordinary Meeting was held in the School on that date at which the Rector gave an address on "St. Monica". Mrs. Cran, whom we are delighted to see well again, hopes to invite us to Rockwood a little later on in the summer. There will be the usual Monthly Meeting on August 3rd, and the Quarterly Service will be held on August 14th. An excursion to Harrogate and Knaresborough has been arranged for July 27th, and will be a thing of the past by the time you read these notes.

ALTAR FLOWERS.

August 7   Mrs. Cran.

    ,,   14   Mrs. Goodall.

    ,,   21   Mrs. & Miss Hanwell.

    ,,   28   The Misses Tarbatt.

BAPTISM.

July 3   Beryl, daughter of Stanley and Barbara Simpson.

BURIALS.

June 28   Thomas Kilner, 82 years.

July 11   Wallace McGregor Morley, 71 years.

The Cumberworth page.

147

HOLY TRINITY CHURCH.

SERVICES FOR AUGUST.

1st   Lammas Day, Holy Eucharist 7 a.m.

4th   S. Dominic, Holy Eucharist 7 a.m.

7th   Eighth Sunday after Trinity—Feast of the Holy Name of Jesus, Holy Eucharist 8 a.m. Procession, Sung Celebration and Sermon 10-30 a.m., followed by Admission of Servers to the Guild of the Servants of the Sanctuary.

11th   Thursday, Holy Eucharist 7 a.m.

14th   Ninth Sunday after Trinity, Holy Eucharist 8 and 10-30 a.m.
First Evensong of the Assumption, Sermon and Procession 6 p.m.

15th   The Assumption of the B. V. M. Celebration of the Holy Eucharist 6 a.m.

21st   Sunday. Holy Eucharist 8 a.m. Sung Celebration and Sermon 10-30 a.m. Preacher, the Rector.
Evensong and Procession 6 p.m. Sermon "The Blessed Virgin and the Emancipation of Woman", Preacher, Curate-in-Charge.

24th   S. Bartholomew, Apostle, Holy Eucharist 7 a.m.

28th   Eleventh Sunday after Trinity— Commemoration of S. Augustine, Bishop, Confessor and Doctor of the Church, Holy Eucharist 8 & 10-30 a.m. Evensong 6 p.m., Sermon: "The Son of S. Monica's Prayers".

29th   Beheading of S. John Baptist, Holy Eucharist 7 a.m.

Mothers' Union.

The Monthly Meeting falls on Wednesday 17, August, that is, within the octave of the festival of the Assumption. This festival is otherwise known as the Dormitio or Falling Asleep of the Blessed Virgin Mary and is so called in the Kalendars of most of the Provinces of the Anglican Communion. The different names correspond to two aspects of the same event. "Falling Asleep", refers to the death to earthly life of the Blessed Virgin. "Assumption" speaks of her entry into Heaven to reign with her everblessed Son, our Saviour and her's.

This great event is the apotheosis of womanhood and naturally provision is made for the due celebration of the final victory of the Second Eve. It is to be hoped that all the women communicants of this congregation will come to the Altar during the festival. Evensong will be sung in the Church on Wednesday, 17th, when we expect all the women whether members of the Mothers' Union or not will attend.

It is not to be thought that men are not also called to worship at this time. Through the obedience of Mary, mankind was enobled by the Eternal Son of God. Men as men and women as women, and all, as children of God, should unite in glorifying God.

Garden Party.

The Rector and Mrs. Taylor have kindly placed the Rectory grounds at our disposal for a Garden Party in aid of Choir funds. The Garden Party will take place on SATURDAY, 20th AUGUST, beginning at 2-30 p.m.

Admission (including Tea) 1/-.

The Choir members will gladly receive gifts and promises of tea, bread, cakes, milk, sugar, butter, etc., etc. Offers of assistance gladly accepted.

A big programme of sports for children will be carried out in the afternoon.

Many novel competitions have been arranged. A dance band will be discourse popular and up-to date music.

Come one! Come all!

The Denby Dale page.

S. John the Evangelist's Church.

The Sale of Work.

This was to have been held out of doors, but owing to the rain was held in the School.

In spite of the wet weather the success of this exceeded the wildest dreams of all. When all has been reckoned up a total profit of well over £90 has been made.

Our best thanks are due to all who worked most enthusiastically. It is difficult to single out any names for special mention as the work of everybody was so splendid. Mr. Norton, in a few well chosen words declared the Sale open.

Lady Hinchliffe very kindly gave the tea. The School proved almost too small for the job, for traffic was very congested.

After tea the girls of the Day School gave a very pretty exhibition of country dances, which were so much enjoyed that a repeat performance was given later.

The result of this great effort augurs well for the future, especially if the same spirit can be kept up.

Below is appended a rough estimate of the above-mentioned profits :—

		£	s	d
T. Norton, Esq.		10	0	0
The Rev. W. A. Taylor ...		1	1	0
Mrs Kenyon			5	0
Tea and Entrance		20	7	8
Jumble Stall ... £7	4 6			
Ice Cream ... 7	0			
Pedlar ... 12	3½			
Gypsies... 10	10½——8	14	8	
Sweet Stall		6	4	8
Miscellaneous Stall		15	0	0
Needlework Stall		25	5	2
Handkerchief, &c., Stall ...		7	8	11
Fruit, Flower, and Vegetable Stall		6	3	3
Hardware Stall		1	19	4
Engine		1	1	0
Bran Tub			13	0
Mrs. Hudson's Cake ...		1	4	4
Tennis Tournament Entry ...			2	0
		£105	10	0
Tickets paid in deducted ...		12	5	0
Grand Total ...		£93	5	0

N.B.—Result partly owing to work done before June 25th, up to which time £53 17 11

had been received and £53 14 11½ paid out. The former includes profits of tea at Working Parties, money for tickets, and payment for orders received. A summer holiday has followed but many orders have yet to be carried out as soon as the Working Parties start again.

The Feast.

There were great doings in Denby at the Feast.

On the Sunday (July 10th), the collections in Church were given to the Sunday School towards the expenses of the Feast.

Monday July 11th, the scholars all met in Church, and after a short service set out for the annual walk round the village, headed by the Denby United Silver Prize Band. There were various stopping places en route at which one or two hymns were sung. This year the walk was rather longer than usul. When the walk was over the scholars, helpers, &c , sat down to a most excellent tea in the school.

It should be mentioned that on that occasion the weather was perfect, about the only time this year when decent weather was experienced. However everybody said that it would be fine for Denby Feast and this year was no exception. Our best thanks are due to all who helped. Again one must comment on the splendid spirit shown by all, and hope that the same excellent spirit may continue.

Below is appended a balance sheet of the proceedings :—

Received.		£	s	d
Collected in the Village... ...		5	9	9
Collected in Church, (July 10th) ...		2	8	3
Total ...		7	18	0

Paid.		£	s	d
Band		4	15	0
Tea, &c.		2	10	0
Total ...		7	5	0

Balance in hand 13/-, (thirteen shillings).

Mothers' Union.

The next meeting of the Mothers' Union will take place on Tuesday August 9th, at 7-15 p m. in the Vicarage,

Congratulations to the following children from the Day School who have gained County Minor Scholarships :—
George Jackson, Hilda Heath, Emily Roebuck, Alice Bell.

The Upper Denby page.

Advertisements from the joint parish magazine of 1927. It is to be wondered as to what happened to the modern sounding 'Sports Depot', as this is the first mention I have ever come across.

150